To my
Favorite cousin(.

I love you so much and am
super thankful you were able
to see us on your visit

May God's light lead you to
experince The Morning Glow!

Love,
Yolanda Luis

THE MORNING
YOU MEET YOU

By

Yolanda Lewis

EXTREME OVERFLOW ENTERPRISES INC., PUBLISHING
GRAYSON, GEORGIA

THE MORNING

YOU MEET YOU

TABLE OF COMMENTS

INTRODUCTION

From the heels of *Shhh, It's a Secret, the Power of Deliverance* and *Expressions, a* poetry and affirmation journal, I have journeyed forward into a place of confidence, peace, and grace. I have pressed into *"The Morning I Met Me."*

I wrote this book during a time of spiritual redefinition, which turned into a personal event of self efficacy. I describe this journey as a press because the expedition to this place of confidence, peace, and grace was no "cake walk."Along this journey there has been plenty of opposition. But, I'm glad that I didn't give up. Persevering on the path to finding peace with what God created me to be, ushered me into a position that no longer needed the approval of others to feel accepted. What a relief this was to discover.

As I stand in the new day's sun I've entered into a place that is constantly secure in moving forward. This was accomplished by first being honest with myself. I asked myself the tough question, why do I feel that I need "their" approval anyway? For years I could not find the answer to this question within myself because for years, I was not willing to face and accept the truthful and appropriate reply. However, change began to occur on the day that

I awoke in my morning. I could no longer hide from the sun. My morning had arrived and illuminated a response so real that its resonation released me from the chains I had let so many people adorn me with. It was at this moment that I realized the answer to the initial tough question was, "I don't."

The reality that made this question so difficult to confront was that I didn't know who I was outside of receiving other people's approval. I believed everything people said about me whether it was good or bad. I embraced it all! When I finally realized that I never needed their approval to begin with, I still felt naked in my realization. In my new found greatness I had no idea what I, was supposed to be looking like. Was it another person to emulate? Although I knew the answer was no, I searched the world anyway. Only later to find out that the look of greatness and approval I was trying to find and eventually become was already who I was within.

As a Christian woman broken by the process and grace of life, I neglected to realize that I was already validated by the Creator of the universe! His approval is the ultimate approval. In understanding this, I also learned to trust Him in a deeper way. I learned to trust Him to navigate my journey but also to walk with me on it. In turn this helped me to understand that my explorative journey was bringing me to a restored sense of "God-fidence."

Through the discovery of myself along this journey to "God-fidence" I learned that for a long time I had allowed feelings of anger, fear, shame, guilt, hurt and lack of trust, define who I was. All of these emotions deafened my ear and ignored my soul cry for an awakening. Deep down inside I wanted to flourish and blossom into a more positive being, but I did not know how or where to begin. So instead these emotions became a very strong part of my reality, a reality that wasn't even true.

The sun in my morning shed light on the dark reasons why I allowed the aforementioned emotions build into feelings of inferiority inadequacy, incompetency and disqualification whenever I did not feel approved or accepted by others; much of which was related to areas of trauma that had not yet been dealt with. Almost unconsciously you too may be allowing the people in your circle to sway your confidence away from the desires God has placed in your heart; simple desires like peace and confidence. All because you have not let the light of the morning expose and awaken you. Other times you may find yourself on a quest to obtain acceptance from others in attempts to dissuade the fear of feeling like a complete failure in life. In either case these same people, whether they are friend or foe, are essentially given permission to drive your life's vehicle. In most cases this class of drivers only uses the rearview mirror as a guide and tricks you into believing you are on the move. You might be on the move alright, moving backward. If this is you, wake up because you may soon be headed for disaster.

There is something to be said about why you might allow other people to drive your life's vehicle instead of the Creator of the universe. Along my journey I have learned that allowing such influence can potentially be steering you away from the manifestation and joy of your life purpose instead of driving you towards it.

Other times it's not people, but life experiences, obligations, or the need to fill our space with busy work (mostly subdued in an over compensation of reality) that can get you side tracked. Regardless, these are the types of distractions that may be successful in pulling you away from God and even farther away from accomplishing your life purpose. Why would you give people or things such authority over YOUR life? That is not God's design.

There is no one who knows you better than your Creator. So why not seek and accept His approval? You may need to ask yourself why God's approval is not validation enough. In doing so, you may uncover some un-contended issues to address. If that happens, it's okay. The dawn of a new morning may reveal "now" as a time to deal with them. In the same way the dawn of a new morning let me know that it was time to kick all of those people, their opinions and the regurgitation of the past out of the driver's seat and replace them with one driver, God. What is the dawn of the new morning saying to you?

Living in the warmth and beauty of the sun rays of self actualizing God-fidence, has revealed and restored to me the importance of taking the time to seek God's map of plan for life. The morning taught me that His path is what can illuminate the best life you could ever imagine. Not because life would emphatically be perfect, but rather it is because of the fulfillment you can discover. The event of the morning afforded me the opportunity to live a life that is not subjective to circumstance, situations or other peoples judgment and opinions.

The event of the morning has a sound. Listen for it. With a hard heart and closed mind, you won't be able to hear the voice of Him that is trying to awake you. When the voice of God awakened me, I took on a renewed sense of significance. I experienced a transformation inside that manifested a burst of spiritual freedom. My hope is that by the end of this book, you will too.

As with any change this process takes time. In the same token, the process involves establishing or for some restoring a relationship with God. As well as being open to His insight. The morning sun can help you to illuminate the truth. The truth is God cannot be put in a box. He has no limitations. And in the power of your morning, neither do you.

This book was written to serve as your personal alarm clock. It's time to wake up and experience your best day ever! May you be awakened to the greatness within. May it awaken your drive, and with Gods power, reveal substantial life purpose. Be awakened by The Morning You Meet You. Now, arise, always knowing that YOUR future... is limitless!

APPROVED

Chapter 1

YOU'RE ALREADY VALIDATED!

Have you ever had a dream that was completely wild and at the time didn't seem to have any meaning; that is, outside of just being plain old weird? Maybe you've experienced a dream that you couldn't forget. When this happens you may want to take into consideration that your dream might mean something.

Morning Realization:

After a long exhausting day, Michelle came home from work and plopped on the couch. Before she knew it, she had fallen into a deep sleep. She began to dream. It all started off with Michelle and her best friend on a beach. In front of them the beach was filled with beautiful white sand and turquoise blue crystal clear water. When the woman looked out on the water it darkened. Naturally the color changed where the oceans depth began. Behind Michelle and her friend was a hill.

The hill was overlaid with white beach sand. Towards the top of the hill was a thick woodsy area. The view was magnificent. The weather was perfect and all types of people were scattered about playing on the beach and lying in the sun. It was a warm summer peaceful day.

As Michelle and her best friend laid on the hilly part of the beach, they started to hear what sounded like trees snapping followed by the thunderous roar of rushing water. The thunderous roar of rushing water was intermingled with screams and people scurrying to try and save their lives. In attempts to avoid the inevitable disaster that was about to occur, Michelle and her best friend screamed and began to run frantically toward the water. They hoped that if they were already in the water when it crashed they would just float with the current and eventually be rescued.

Michelle's best friend bolted ahead of her. As Michelle began to run, all of the frenzy behind her quieted. Michelle continued to run. In the midst of the chaos, Michelle heard a voice. The voice said, "Don't run. Let the current take you." So Michelle stopped running and asked out loud, "Don't run?" At that very second Michelle stopped running and the rushing water behind her took her in its grasp.

Michelle watched many people drown while she was being pushed by the water current, to include her best friend. Michelle watched her best friend's body fight for life. The current was too strong and did not allow Michelle to save her friend. She heard a voice again that said, "Don't look back." Michelle wiped the tears from her eyes (from seeing her best friend drown) and faced forward.

The water had risen high and had darkened in color. It was as if Michelle was standing in a bottomless body of water surrounded by other people. She recognized the other people as friends who were riding the waves with her. Although they were riding the waves collectively they were floating in separate groups. These groups were moving quickly, as if they were traveling on a cement paved highway. Similar to how you would travel on the road when driving on a paved highway, Michelle found her friends within the groups taking "exits" off of the "highway" on to dry land. Not all of the groups of friends took the same exit, however they did all take an exit that led them to dry land. Even still other people were swimming for their life nearby, while others were floating waiting for help.

As she passed many familiar faces and looks of desperation, Michelle heard the voice again saying, "Don't look back." Michelle wanted to look back because she didn't know what to expect ahead. She was trying to forecast what her end may look like based off of what she saw others experiencing. Michelle was afraid to travel on the water "highway" by herself. Although Michelle watched each of her friends take the "exits," she wondered when it was going to be her turn to take the exit. She heard the voice again. The voice said, "Don't look back." So Michelle didn't look back again. Instead she looked down.

The ocean floor seemed to be miles away. This struck fear in Michelle because she was moving really fast. She couldn't help but think, "What if I drown?" When she looked around, she realized that there was no one around to answer her question. She heard nothing from the voice that had been guiding her. Michelle started to become lonely. She had reached the part of her journey where there were no more friends traveling with her. It was just Michelle and the water. This made her feel anxiously frustrated. Michelle started to wonder if or when she was ever going to get to dry land. She became even more afraid when she looked beneath her only to find that the water color was even darker than before. It was navy blue in color. It almost looked black.

Michelle floated for a while in the water, alone. Until it was all of a sudden that the waters seemed to calm. With the water calmed Michelle could now see the shore. She had finally reached the point where she was close enough to swim to shore. The shore was another beach and it was nearly empty. But Michelle swam with all of her might and with rest on her mind. Even though she was getting tired she continued to swim anyway. She felt that she was too close to land to quit.

By this point, it had been a long journey with many loses to include friends and strength. Michelle was exhausted. Then it seemed as though there was less and less water to swim in. Michelle turned around only to find the water drew back and formed a huge wave; a tsunami sized wave. So she held her breath. The wave was getting ready to crash right on top of her. Despite her best efforts Michelle could not swim fast enough to get away from the wave that was about to crash. The wave crashed on her in full force and washed her up on shore.

Finally ashore, Michelle crawled on her hands and knees up to the sand while breathing heavily. Her eyes were closed in fatigue. Michelle was depleted of energy. Voices began to surround her and chatter. She heard the voices say, "Who is she?" "Where did she come from?" "Wow..." Michelle resumed strength enough to open her eyes. When she opened her eyes she looked at her hands. From her knees Michelle sat back on her legs and saw something unfamiliar. Her hands were sparkling like someone poured glitter on them. Michelle didn't even recognize her own hands because they were sparkling. Although perplexed Michelle was intrigued by her sparkling hands. Strangely enough, she liked how they looked.

As she lifted her head she saw shadows of people and a very bright light. This new group of people surrounded her as she lifted herself up. Once on her feet, Michelle then woke up.

Typically if you can remember your dream it usually means something. Sometimes it could mean you ate too many sweets too late the night before. While other times your dre[...]

way of speaking directly to you.

The dream described was about a woman's journey to accepting herself and her journey as her own. Additionally it was about trusting the voice that was guiding her and not being afraid to listen to the voice, despite the tumultuous circumstances the woman was going through; circumstances that seemed to change constantly. Furthermore this dream was symbolic to the event of a personal awakening; representational to the morning you meet you.

GUIDING VOICE

On your journey to the morning you meet you, it is important to trust the voice of God and the place where He is guiding you. If you don't know what the voice of God sounds like, you can try to listen for it in a quiet place. Perhaps you don't have a physical quiet place to go to. You may have so many things going on in your world where it may feel like even silence is screaming at you. Nevertheless, God can still speak to you and your situation because He loves you. You may have to listen hard, but listen all the same. God loves you so much that sometimes he will turn on sirens, flashing lights, and booming bright fireworks just to get your attention. He wants you to hear His voice, so try to do your best not to miss it. It will be over time and through various experiences at you will learn what the voice of God sounds like to you. As you grow closer and learn more about Him, you can find his voice to be comforting, soothing and trustworthy. Try your best to listen carefully, patiently, and quietly.

CONFIDENCE IN SOLITUDE

While the voice of God can guide you throughout the lifetime of your journey there are other relationships that are not meant to last forever. You may have had to learn how to let go of people and leave them in the past. It is important to understand this concept. There will be some relationships that are a part of your life to help you for a reason and a season. In either regard, you must learn not to give the permanent power of influence to people that have temporary existence in your life. If you do, you may end up holding onto relationships that only serve as dead weight to your future. Maybe you have been the one left holding the emotional baggage. In either instance, let the past be the past. In the case of the latter, put the bags down!

Relationship endings are not always negative. Sometimes you may just lose touch. Other times the closeness you once shared may dissipate. That is ok. You can still let go or move on even if there wasn't anything negatively dramatic ending the relationship. Have you found yourself in a relationship where the season was long overdue, yet you still looked to the relationship for a sense of belonging or approval? Have you ever felt the need to hang on to a relationship because you felt it needed you? If so you may be dealing with a deeper issue relative to an inaccurate sense of self.

ALREADY VALIDATED

An inaccurate sense of self warps the psychological and spiritual perspectives of the healthy interactivity of your inner self. This means that you may either be over or under inflating or deflating your value, extremely. Furthermore an inaccurate sense of self distracts from the true healing that can come from the death of unhealthy or in this case ending relationships. Those who have an accurate sense of self have a balanced comprehension and acceptance of themselves which frees them to experience a greater emotionally and spiritually healthy life style (McMinn, 1996). If you are a person who does not have a healthy sense of self, you may also feel that a sense of approval is subsequently missing.

According to Webster's dictionary, a seal of approval is a stamp or certification. A stamp of approval can enable you to feel a sense of validation. This type of validation can make you feel important. Everyone wants and needs to feel important. What are the things that make you feel important?

Obtaining a stamp of approval from others, promises to give a temporary satisfaction to your lack of contentment within. Your need to be accepted should not outweigh or subtract from the sufficiency being accepted by God offers. The reality is the power and ability to change lives or stamp someone as approved belongs to your Creator, and no one else. Since God has already validated you and has your best interest in mind, it is now up to you to embrace it.

> *"No eye has seen no ear has heard no mind has conceived what God has prepared for those who love him but God has revealed it to us by his Spirit."*   *1 Corinthians 2:9-10*

This scripture is indicative to the fact that the future God has in store for you is bigger than you can ever imagine. It is even better than any plan you could put in place on your own. Most importantly what God has in store for you is exclusive to your personality, character and skills. All you have to do is believe that there is better and accept that a part of your journey's responsibility is to reach for the better. Accepting your journey may cause you to face some challenges. However the reward will bring you to a place of newness, peace, and inspiration.

Look around, are you surrounded by people who don't believe there is a better future for you just ahead? Have you been looking for approval from people, places, or situations and not seeking the approval from the Creator of the Universe? Are you consumed by the negativity of your current situation? Have you lost hope? If you answered yes to any of these questions, it may be time to experience an awakening. The accomplishment this awakening can bring can surround you with newness, peace and inspiration as you begin to realize God's approval as complete validation.

Living a life within the limitations of other people's expectations when you don't know who you are will drive you insane and keep you bound to feel trapped in a box. It will leave you longing for people and things that are insignificant. However, realizing God's purpose for your life and accepting the journey therein is a step of empowerment towards finding true validation and discovering that your morning is truly already APPROVED!

Chapter 1

Tips and Helpful Hints to Remember

- God validated your presence on this earth the day you were born. You are here on purpose and to do great things.
- Your journey is unique - embrace it.
- Don't give people or things validating power that does not belong to them.

Be Inspired:

Believe in yourself and all that you are. Know that there is something inside you greater than any obstacle.

-Christian D. Larson

Meditate on this:

And we know that in all things God works for the good of those who love him, who have been called according to his purpose.

-Romans 8:28

Repeat this Affirmation of Encouragement:

I am approved by God and I trust that He is leading me to achieve my highest good, now.

REINVENTION

REVITALIZE YOUR CHARACTER WITH NEW PURPOSE

Metaphorically, you may have endured earthquakes, floods and all types of natural disasters life can bring about. When these storms hit sometimes the only thing left to do is rebuild, as in reinvent.

Morning Realization:

> Michelle was running late to meet her girlfriends for their regularly scheduled end of the week dinner. She couldn't wait to tell them about her crazy dream as well as share some pretty awkward news. Although the news was indeed gauche, she had no doubt in her mind that her friends would be available to support her during such a life crisis. Michelle had always supported her friends no matter how foolish their choices may have been.

When she arrived at the restaurant her girlfriends were very glad to see her. To get the night started they ordered her favorite alcoholic drink. Michelle declined which sent her girlfriends into frenzy. "Michelle, since when do you turn down a drink? We always toast to the end of a hard week," said Janice. Michelle sat down and took a deep breath. She responded by letting the girls know the reason why she could not have a drink. "I'm pregnant." "You're what?" Janice said. "How could you do that?" Nicky echoed. Michelle now uncomfortable and embarrassed gave the best answer she could. "Well it wasn't planned. You all know I have lots on my plate. This was not in the plan at all." Michelle's nervous laughter filled the air and was quickly evaporated by the judgmental thoughts of her friends.

There was a brief moment of silence before Debbie interrupted the quiet roar of emotions. "So who is the guy?" Michelle's friends anxiously awaited her response. However Michelle was trying very hard to be engrossed in the menu. She holds back the tears that are ready to flood her face and says, "The maintenance man. I know how this sounds..." All of Michelle's friends gasp with disgust. They are infuriated by her response. They each abruptly interject, "The maintenance man!" "You couldn't do any better than that, Michelle" "This is the biggest mistake of your life!"

Michelle couldn't hold back the tears any longer, so she let them flow. Amongst her tears none of her friends tried to console her. "So, let me get this straight," said Nicky, "You mean to tell me your boyfriend is the maintenance man?" After a brief pause all of the girlfriends laughed until they noticed that Michelle was not laughing. "So you're serious?" Debbie says. Michelle, with her head down, nodded as a reply. All of the friends looked at each other in pure repulsion. Nicky began to put her coat on. "This is ridiculous," she said. "Not only did you ruin your life, you just ruined our ladies night dinner. I'm out of here." Michelle is now shocked and responds in irritation. "At the moment I need you guys the most, you're going to just up and leave, Nicky? Just like that, huh? And after all these years?" Michelle cannot believe her friends response. "I agree with Nicky, I think it's time to go. Let's go Janice." With tears in her eyes and confusion circling her thoughts, Michelle couldn't stop her emotions from pouring out. "If you all cannot value our friendship to weigh more than any decision I make, whether you agree or not that's fine with me. I will take care of this child by myself." "By yourself? Do you realize what you're saying," Janice said. "You have no idea what it takes to be a mother," Debbie cosigned. "What happened to our commitment to staying clear of children until we got married?" Kim asked. Michelle is now exasperated. "Are you talking about that silly pack we made fifteen years ago? We are thirty-five year old adult women who are fully capable of being responsible for the choices we make. I still can't even believe the ludicrousness of your reaction. I am completely baffled and wonder after all of this time, whether or not our friendship meant anything to you at all."

Nicky has her coat on and is now paying the check. But she chimed in to add her two cents. "All I know is that you've violated our pack. You've isolated yourself to be on a completely separate level. I don't think I can support that." Michelle is flabbergasted and responds in rebuttal, "You're right; I am on a new level now. And to think that I thought I could find comfort in our bond after being utterly dismissed by the baby's father." Kim erupted in laughter before she spoke, "Girl, you are crazy. Much crazier than I thought." Michelle looked stunned and appalled. She was just about to give a pretty nasty comeback before being interrupted, yet again, "Wait, before you say anything I'll say it for you." Nicky moved closer to Michelle's ear to ensure that she could hear every word that she was about to say. "You can take your baby, deadbeat baby's father and your new level and forget we ever met. You can make a mess in your life, all by yourself because you know better." These words were like daggers being driven in Michelle's heart. Nicky stood up and continued, "Ladies, I think we're done here."

Michelle picks up her heart from the floor and swallows her pride while she is left sitting alone in the restaurant watching all of her friends walk out on her.

Reinvention can happen for various reasons. Some instances are because you may have accomplished a set of goals and it's time to create new ones. Maybe your last child recently graduated high school. Or maybe you have just finished college or just had a baby. These defining moments can be a joyous time to discover reinvention. While other times, personal reinvention may be inspired by a loss. Perhaps you have lost a friend or a job. Maybe you are recently divorced or a loved one has passed away. While these types of defining moments can be sad, the reinvention of you can serve to be quite exhilarating.

This may be one of the few times in life where reinventing the wheel might be your best option. Reinventing yourself has everything to do with your character. The revitalization of your character will establish and for some restore a new sense of purpose. After the storms of life have hit, reinventing your self will be the vice that re-cessitates your life. Naturally that sounds so easy, right?

This grassroots concept of inventing or for some reinventing self can be an experience shared within the constant cyclical progression of: Reveal, Revive, Redefine, and Conquer.

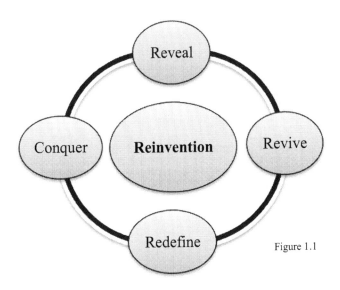

Figure 1.1

The diagram above expresses the evolution a person might experience as it relates to efficacious growth and development; towards aspirations such as new dreams, new goals and in essence a new life! This developmental growth can be journeyed in stages.

THE REVEAL STAGE recognizes the need for change and its eminence. How will you know when it's time for change? You will know it's time for change when you have outgrown your surroundings. This heightened awareness of growth does not in any way imply that you are better than anyone else. Be careful to halt your imagination at the onset of such selfish thoughts. When you recognize the need for change you're admitting that your clothes don't fit anymore. Maybe your clothes are too tight, too short or too big. In either regard, they are uncomfortable and it's time to take them off; change attire.

Picture it this way, can you imagine wearing a newborns t-shirt as an adult? Aside from uncomfortable, you would look humorously ridiculous! Yet, sometimes people are so afraid of the change event that they'd rather wear clothes that don't fit instead of exploring an entirely new mall to shop at. This is what the reveal stage is all about. Revealing the growth you have experienced and embracing the need to adjust yourself to that growth.

What should you expect throughout your change event? During your change event you can expect change and lots of it! But don't be afraid, the changes you experience may not at all be negative. Fear plays such a tremendous role in the degree to which a person will expose themselves to change. This in many instances can be crippling. Instead of protecting yourself, which is what fear innately will have you believe you are doing, you are limiting your perspective. You might even be choking the life out of your future.

Fear can be paralyzing, but do your best not to allow it to paralyze you during your change event.

Why does change need to happen? You may be thinking, "I'm fine the way I am." If you are, than this is excellent! However if you are not, you may want to think of change in a different light. Change is an essential part of life so long as you live. It is a wedded component to the success of creating a new you. It is also the sustaining element of division between the exploration of what you can be and what you will be. As long as you are alive, change can be one of the most beautiful ceremonies of your life. Try your best to focus on the positive and enjoy the matrimonial union between you and change rather than dreading it.

Will changing yourself hurt? Change does hurt sometimes. But the sting of change is not like touching a hot stove leaving a scar often permanent. Its tenderness can be found in the discomfort of facing the present-day you. The processes full exposure meets God in the deepest secret place of your heart and unveils the treasure, insight and virtue within. The pain dissolves as long as you are willing to confront it.

Confrontation does not have to start nor end as a negative experience. It is simply the process of addressing the issues. If you are a person who does not like confrontation it may feel as though it endures for a long time. Try not to be fixated on the idea of time. Time is relative. The process is what is most important. Confrontation is a part of that process, but God can walk through it with you.

Can a two-man job be done alone? No, this is why two people are needed (for a two-man job). Creating a new version of you can be thought of in the same way. Understanding that your process requires a power and a strength that only God has to offer will help you to be most successful on your journey to self efficacy. God's unlimited wisdom, power and love are essential in this process of change, try to do your best to embrace it.

THE REVIVE STAGE is all about getting excited! Embarking upon a new adventure has a way of introducing great enthusiasm. Similar to the rush you may have felt at Christmas time as a child right before you opened your first gift or on a birthday when your favorite guests begin to arrive. This step is all about drawing energy from a different outlook and attitude while disassociating negativity from your change event. Then, allowing the idea of change to manifest itself as hope!

The energy you draw may even cause you to feel excitedly overwhelmed by the numerous possibilities ahead of you! All of which may be followed by countless opportunities to try new things. Embrace this energy and change forward!

THE REDEFINE STAGE is about seeing a vision of you in a future state, right now. Liken to an artist who sits down and turns lines into sketches and sketching in to drawings and drawings into paintings and paintings into color filled life. Redefining yourself holds the same concept in that it allows you to redraw, re-sketch and repaint a new you by revisiting your beliefs, values and priorities. The entire event of change is not selfish to you and your needs. It is about finding a way to be ok with you in the world you live in. It may mean for you to consider changing your circle of friends. It may also mean for you to learn about how to appreciate the differences in other people and explore how to enjoy the way they compliment your gifts and talents. Within this stage if you find that you are not as strong as you thought; look at these revelations as a great opportunity to reestablish what is important in your life.

With the end goal of yourself in mind, you now hold a responsibility to follow that vision. Following it, means that you believe it in your heart and commit to practicing that belief, by speaking positively to it. You might be the only one who sees this new and improved future self. That is ok. Even if you are the only one who sees it, continue to speak great things to yourself, about yourself and about your future. If you can see it, believe it. Then put its manifestation into practice. By doing so you are being obedient to the instruction God's divinity is directing you towards. He wants you to be and do great things!

Obedience is a sure way to reap success. What you are doing when you are being obedient to God's instruction is practicing the power of love. Love and trust for God. In this sense, the display of your love for God becomes one with your level of obedience to God. Therefore the redefine step in its most capable form is saturated in an unconventional source of love. Where does the source of this love come from?

Do you know anyone who bakes really well? You may have a great baker in your family. The cake recipe they use may taste so good that it makes you want to eat the entire cake in one sitting! Your relative may be known for their ability to make cakes that are insanely incredible. Maybe you've tried to emulate this great recipe and have failed. While your cake may have tasted good, it still might seem as though there was something missing. The special ingredient your family member might be using is one that you cannot buy at the store or borrow from a neighbor. More than likely what makes your relatives cakes especially spectacular is the love added to each step. Love makes the difference not only in cake recipes but it makes the difference in life. Learning about love is one of the key factors within this recreation process.

In the bible there is a story about Jesus talking to the Jewish Religious leaders about the power of love (Mark 12:30-31). The religious leaders Jesus was talking to had made up several laws (six hundred and thirteen to be exact) by this time (in the scripture). These religious leaders were trying to categorize the laws into major and minor laws. Others would argue that it was dangerous to even attempt to differentiate which laws were equally binding. So they asked Jesus for his perspective. Jesus explained to the religious leaders a very simple point. He said that if you love God and love others as you would your own self; you will fulfill the intent of the Ten Commandments as well as other laws. What does that mean? It means that love needs to be seen in all of the things you do and say. It means to love is to be obedient. Redefining the meaning and power of love in your life will actualize a healthy relationship with God and others.

Loving yourself and learning to love other people can help you to better understand how special you are to God. The flow of a redefined love will affirm that what people have said to you or even have said about you truly matter's less and less. In 2008 Coach Bobby Bowden of Florida State University, said it profoundly:

> *"Your reputation is what people say about you, however your character is what God knows about you."*

What people may have said or thought about you does not determine your value and cannot share in any attitudes dictating how you treat others. What you feel about yourself determines your inimitable value. Do you feel good about yourself right now? Perhaps you've made some poor life decisions, so what! Maybe it is time to reinvent. The bottom line and guiding principle is that even after you have fallen, God is still falling in love with you. He sacrificed himself just for you! His love toward you is everlasting.

Everlasting love indicates love for a very long time. Most people do not share everlasting love; they share a conditional love. Or some may not let themselves love past self made limitations of love. However, when you are referring to the love of God, try to think of love on a different level. God's love is infinite and dwells in the infinite realm. The infinite realm is the realm where love is continuous, evolving and has no depth or ceiling or conditions. It is unlimitedly infinite. Infinite love cannot hurt you. God's love is infinite. It cares for you and always has your best interest in mind.

If the only love you've known has hurt and bruised you, you may want to try another kind of love. Try God's love. Loving God first also loves His creation and is indicative to loving yourself. Where is your love level today? Do you love yourself? Without love the foundation of your character will turn into an empty void. You will be as hollow as the echoes in the Grand Canyon, without a redefined sense of love. Therefore the discovery of what love really means to you can find loves pure abundance.

Love it or not, throughout difficult times you may find that what you really may be going through is a character building exercise. During such exercises you are learning how to conquer which is to know better so you can do better.

THE CONQUER STAGE is a reflection of the triumphant you. When will you know that you have arrived here? Sometimes you can experience anxious frustration in waiting on your moment of complete change to arrive. Have you ever gotten lost and needed direction? Did you have to wait for your relief to arrive? Almost like waiting for a bus at a bus stop. You may begin waiting with many other people. You may even watch others pass you by. You might even get tired of waiting alone. However during your reinvention cycle it is true that you might very well explore learning how to wait. Learning how to wait is also learning how to listen; listening for direction and instruction from God. This is a good skill to learn, listening and waiting.

To truly conquer in triumph is going to require you to exhaust your best efforts. Try to find the positive in your waiting. When the morning sun awakens you, you will not be able to doubt its presence. The illumination of a higher sense of self can increase your ability to live a more fulfilled life. That is, if you allow waiting to be a considerate part of the journey. Think of it this way, when you place a seed into the ground, it does not immediately pop up in its full potential. No! There is a process; a process cultivated by nurture and patient, methodical development. If you do get impatient, don't worry. Overtime there is a strong possibility that you experience the patience of God, even in your eagerness. He is careful to love you still. In His infinite love He can carry you through your toughest times. Receiving the light of His love allows you to conquer the reinvention cycle.

Whatever your need may be, God is able to love you through it. It doesn't matter what you may have gone through, His love is available to heal even the deepest wounds. He will love you through sickness of any kind; physical, mental and emotional. He can even heal a broken heart. In the greatest representation of love God endured pain, agony, and persecution, just for you. As an example of love He endured death on a cross so that you can experience real love. God's love is real and unconditional. Unconditional love is the same love you should give yourself.

Reinventing yourself is an intimate experience. The intimacy within is a reflection of God's love for you and thus an instruction of how to love yourself. The process of reinvention identifies faults, wounds and strengths. The outcome is victoriously serene in purification that purges the soul and digs up the root of everything insignificant you held dear. What remains is illuminated by the light of the sun. While this next level of peace is established it won't come without a challenge, and you must rise above it.

Tips and Helpful Hints to Remember

- Consider the fact that it may be time to reinvent yourself.
- Accept God's love and love without limitations.
- Let patience work its virtue.

Be Inspired:

"Reinvention does not indicate failure, it indicates growth."

- Yolanda Lewis

Meditate on this:

"Your beauty should not come from outward adornment... Instead, it should be that of your inner self...."

1 Peter 3: 3, 4

Repeat this Affirmation of Encouragement:

I am loved in God's pure abundance.

The Challenge

Chapter 3

RISING ABOVE

Rising above requires you to think big. It requires you to step on doubts, squash insecurities and leap over any obstacle life presents. Rising above resembles the awakening of the giant inside of you. The challenge to this type of arousal is that it requires an inward transformation; a personal alteration that cannot be faked. The onset of this inward transformation begins when you no longer see yourself or your dreams as small.

Small minded vision permits the giant inside of you to remain asleep intimidated by the potential greatness waiting to explode from within. If you see yourself as small others will view you as the same. To avoid small minded vision you must rise above.

Rising above is realizing that you are bigger than your current circumstances, no matter what they may be.

CLEAR VIEW

When you first meet you, you may feel invincible. You may feel free and empowered. You might even feel the sunrise kiss your soul and smile as a new you is birthed. However the more clearly you begin to see and feel the new you emerge, the more friends you might seem to be losing. The people who you once called your friend may start vanishing right before your eyes. It is during this time that you will learn the difference between a real friend and the people you have just always had around and called your friend.

Over time the absence of clarity can reveal how distinctly different these categories are. Once you realize the distinction between a real friend and a familiar friend, then the next challenge you may discover is learning how to let one of them go.

RELEASE

If you start to lose familiar friends, understand it may not be because you did something wrong. You may have days where you feel stunned shock. You might even feel like asking God, "What did I do that was so terrible to be the only one feeling such a loss?" Don't buy into this cheap fantasy and naively avoid its blatant truth. You may not be the one at a loss. The challenge then is grasping this concept as truth. Even in situations where your character is being challenged, the loss of familiar friends is an indication that you are in a new level movement; moving to a new plateau in your journey to discover self. The release of some relationships can help you transition your vision. This vision shift can facilitate dream flow ability in the experience of seeing yourself live the greatest life you've ever imagined. Are you living in a world that has become too small for your giant sized dream? If so, accept and embrace the changes that come during this process.

AMAZING GRACE

Have you ever been in a situation where you had to face something you felt you couldn't deal with? If so then you probably were in need of something you didn't have. Even still, God's grace is sufficient. Throughout your process you may find the need for God's extra special grace. God's grace is a supernatural power, that's why it is called amazing. God will make sure you always have what you need. Whatever is removed from your life rest assure He can replace it with something more fitted to your new destiny. The challenge is to be open and flexible to receiving the new; which can be people places or things.

With God you don't always get what you deserve. In most cases you get exactly what you do not deserve, God's best. The law teaches that you should only get what you deserve. The law does not teach grace. Thankfully, God doesn't operate that way. God always gives his very best. Unlike the law, God loves his children. Therefore there is no need to hide from him in guilt or shame of your past. Hiding from Him suggests that the principles of the law are more powerful than that of God's supernatural grace. With God you are debt free. Thus, the reason to feel ashamed or guilty of the past is obsolete. In all else, God's grace is sufficient. The challenge then is to receive God's grace along the processing of your journey.

POWERFUL NOT POWERLESS

Perhaps you might experience a different challenge. Maybe you struggle with feeling powerless to change because you have lost hope in life. Your challenge then, is to find a way to believe in hope or believe in hope again. Think about your life. In most cases you have already overcome even the worst of situations which God may have used in preparing you to do what others are afraid to even consider. However, don't be afraid to walk in your greatness, embrace it! What God wants you to do he'll give you the power to accomplish. Hope and believe again! Embracing your greatness is embracing your journey. All you have to do is accept the challenge to rise above.

The challenge to rise above is an action. You must walk it out; even if that means to walk away from people, places or things. The quicker you learn how to embrace this challenge is the quicker you will grow into your giant sized future. It may take you awhile to grab hold of understanding that the absence of the people, places or things you are used to may actually be a direct result of the transition that is occurring in your life, and not a result of anything negative. While you may be alone and feel as though you are losing a lot, you are not. Everyone is not supposed to grow with you to your next level. Essentially, what you are experiencing is a shedding called, new level movement.

NEW LEVEL MOVEMENT

Navigating through the dynamics of a new level movement can be pretty demanding, never mind the idea of having to pass through these levels alone. Despite the odds and with all of your strength, try to remain focused and careful during this time. Use careful conscience thought regarding what you say, choosing your words wisely. The words that come out of your mouth are so critical during your new level movement. In the power of your essence you hold the opportunity to alter the progress therein if you choose to let your emotions get the best of you. Make a supreme effort to speak life instead of death to yourself and your situation.

As you are rising above, the deliberate action of speaking life means that you are making a conscience decision to undergo a character surgery. This surgery may include changing your perception from being people focused to God centered. Being people focused is caring more about what other people say and think over your own thoughts and opinions. More notably, over God's as well. This is not as hard to avoid as you may think.

Morning Realization:

Michelle goes through a bout of depression and loneliness. She has been going over in her mind the last meeting she had with her friends and is even contemplating abortion. Michelle has sent weekly text messages to her girlfriends trying to apologize for any rudeness that she may have displayed. She also offered another opportunity to talk under more reasonable and supportive mindsets. She is worried and afraid for her future and has received no response from her friends.

Michelle felt as sad as the weather looked outside of her bedroom window. The rain beat on her window as the sun hid behind the clouds. She felt like she wanted to give up. She looked at her phone as she fell to the floor. Still, she had not received any response from her friends. Feeling extremely weak, Michelle slumped over the edge of her bed for support and just wept. While she is crying she feels something around her. Almost as if someone was giving her a hug. She cried some more. She was distraught and hadn't eaten for at least two days.

As a school teacher, she was now out of work for the summer. Michelle had nothing but time on her hands all of which is being consumed by her situation. All of a sudden she received a text message from Nicky which read, "Listen, I know I was really harsh toward you when I saw you a month ago. But what did you expect me to say? I've been talking to the girls and some of my coworkers and they all agree that your decision to have this baby is the worst choice you could ever make. I'll go with you to get rid of it and get your life back. Let me know." Michelle read every word in disbelief. She also began to feel anger rising up. She started to write back, but then received another text message from Kim. "Hey Shelly, I accept your apology. I'm over it now, even though you were tripping, girl. Nicky told us she was going to talk to you last week about some options. Hoping you're better now. Call me."

"Are you serious?" Michelle yelled as she blurted out her rhetorical question. Michelle shook her head as she came to the sudden realization that she had been wasting her time in trying to explain herself to women who were clearly stuck in their own ways. She decided that she would reply to Nicky for the last time, "If that was your idea of an apology, you can keep it. I've made my decision. But thanks anyway." Michelle decided that she would also reply to Kim one last time as well, "Thanks." After sending the text messages, Michelle stood up from her bedside and sat at the window seat in her bedroom.

Michelle made the decision to just accept things as they were. She took a deep breath and felt peace as she stared at the hustle and bustle going on underneath her downtown condo.

The evidence was clear, two of her friends didn't even respond to her apology, while the other two either accepted her apology in vain or didn't accept the apology at all by way of ignoring the issue. But Michelle decided that she was ok with this and would move forward.

Shortly after enjoying the peace and quiet of her thoughts, Michelle started to receive numerous text messages, now from each of her girlfriends. She started to read the messages but then decided to stop and put the phone down. Devastated by the fact that they were all seemingly conspiring against her and had been talking about her to various other people behind her back, Michelle decided that this was not the life she wanted to live or be a part of. Therefore she opted not to answer any more of the messages and quickly called her phone company to change her phone number.

Think about the last dispute or disagreement you had. Did you speak positively? Could you resist the implosion of selfish fulfillment? In your response, were you people focused, self centered or God focused? Remembering the promise of your future can easily get lost in the translation of a heated argument. Have you ever spent countless hours trying to explain yourself? If so you might have found that you were explaining yourself to people who either don't matter or don't really care. Realize this, at the end of any day you don't owe anyone an explanation for where you've been in life, where you are at (in life) or where you are going (in life). People who do not want to see you succeed do not share the same mind as you. This is why you cannot get on their level and begin explaining yourself. These type of people are happy to try and make you feel bad about your progression. But do not pay these people any mind. They don't understand your process and really they don't have to. You on the other hand should be perfectly clear about your journey of destiny. Being perfectly clear doesn't mean that you will know or even agree with every turn, or change that awaits you along the journey. It just means you have committed to trusting God's design for it and the success therein the process. If you are still trying to explain yourself to everyone, you may want to consider whether or not you have found true contentment in your journey.

If people want to judge you for where you are today, or the mistakes you have made yesterday, who cares? Let them wait at the bus stop of negativity by themselves. Just because they haven't caught the vision or do not believe you will get to a place of success does not put you in debt of explaining your plan or your process to them. If you find it difficult to strike a balance between what is best to say and to whom, it might be a good idea for you to keep your thoughts and comments to yourself until you are more confident. Sometimes your response can give negative people the ammunition needed to shoot you down. Despite the fact that negative people are going to judge you anyway, do your best not to give them the stones to crucify you with. Avoid this temptation at all costs.

It can be difficult to understand the idea of waiting patiently when you want change right away. Sometimes you may feel so excited about your progress that you want to share it with everyone. Even the people you know couldn't care less. If you find yourself in this position ask yourself, what are you trying to prove, to whom, and why? The challenge and beauty of your journey is personal. Let your journey speak for itself! No public service announcements are necessary! You owe it to yourself to be content with your journey. The challenge is to accept that your journey will all make sense when it's supposed to.

NO REGRETS, ONLY LESSONS LEARNED

Have you ever done something you wish you never did? Or maybe you've experienced words running so fast away from your lips that you said some things you only wish you could take back? Maybe you even over judged someone you knew nothing about? When you begin to grow and realize how much and how many times you may have hurt people because of your own seared emotions, you might feel awful and want to ask everyone for forgiveness. When you are on your way to do this, one important thing to remember is that just because you are ready to forgive and move forward, others may not be at the same place. This doesn't mean that you are better than anyone else. It just means that they aren't ready. The challenge is to accept this and learn to move past needing their forgiveness if they choose not to forgive you.

Forgiving yourself can be the hardest part of rising above. Forgiveness is a forward thinking action. Forgiving yourself is confronting feelings of guilt, remorse and shame. It is then an act of letting it all go, accepting the experience and separating the old you from the new you. Forgiveness is being ok with who you are, what you've done, and where you're going. Forgiveness is accepting the lessons learned without punishing yourself. The challenge of forgiving yourself sets you free. When you forgive, you can leave the negative behind. Remember, you don't live there anymore!

In some cases pride may be standing in front of the desire to conform to an apology. However, the process of forgiving yourself may require you to reach out and apologize to others. After you've pushed the wall of pride down, what if they don't want your apology? What if your realization to apologize comes too late? The reality is sometimes people just won't or don't want to forgive you. People will try to get you to repay them for forever. It is extremely important to make the decision to move past the need to be forgiven by others, after you've done your part. If you buy into schemes of unforgiveness you are engaging in dysfunction. Sure you may feel remorseful; this is a healthy part of taking ownership for the offense. But it is an unhealthy notion for others to expect you to stay there forever. Allowing this behavior to operate in your life is like giving these people the rope to choke you with. As a willful participant whose remorse is being taken advantage of, you are aiding in your own crucifixion. This type of crucifixion seeks to choke the life out of you so that you never move forward in forgiving again. Choking you is the same as muting your voice. If your voice is mute then it cannot speak of positivity. Speaking in positive form allows you to operate in forgiveness where speaking negatively in un-forgiveness only halts you from being able to move forward from the offense. Your voice is also the instrument used to call forth your purpose. Your destiny is the path you take to fulfill it. Therefore a crucifixion eliminates the power to move forward in calling your purpose and reaching destiny. The challenge will be not to let anyone take your voice from you. Even if it means accepting that the person you offended does not want your apology.

No matter how much you may try, you cannot make people forgive you. Further you cannot make people see how sorry you are, or that you are different now or even that you recognize the hurt you may have caused them. Matter of fact, they may not even care! Just as truth cannot be forced, liken to an apology forgiveness can only be accepted or declined. Some people may even feel better leaving things in complete disarray; without any possibility of closure. Others may rather hold a grudge against you. However, whether they choose to forgive you or they choose not to forgive you is rightfully their prerogative. You however are not obligated to take part in accepting the invitation to any manipulative piteous parties. Whatever their reasoning, you can move forward. Moving forward then is a decision, not a complexity.

OUT OF CONTROL

Do you tend to make things complex unnecessarily? Why? There
is no reason to overcomplicate things in the process of rising
above. If you are able to make a truce, by all means apologize and
restore important relationships. Apologizing is an important part of
the process. However the process doesn't stop if the person doesn't
receive your apology. A genuine apology can do wonders for your
soul and for the victim.

Also, it is a key point to be careful not to become a casualty of just
doing the right thing because something is the right thing to do. No
matter how good you are at tricking everyone else, you cannot
trick yourself. If your apology is insincere it can return with a
vengeance. The authentic you will always peak its face in these
types of situations. The prideful wicked head of insincerity may
cause further damage in the future to you or the relationship you
are trying to reconcile. In the same token, do your best not to let
pride become the death of you. Instead humble yourself and
sincerely apologize.

Humbling your thoughts helps to quiet the roar of chaos sometimes
going on in your mind. Furthermore, humility helps to avoid the
unnecessary stress of a prideful nature. Pride leads to restlessness
because it highlights a comparison of you to others. In comparison

to others, pride makes you think that you are better than everyone else. When you compare yourself to others, it can cause you to be concerned with stuff that may not matter in the grand scheme of things. It can cause you to become driven to prove a point instead of being driven to enjoy life. By contrast, humility allows you to accept your journey and celebrate others. Such contentment gives you security so that you no longer have to compare yourself to others because you are satisfied with who you are and the journey therein.

When you rise above, it can be a challenge to focus on the things you have going on with a positive attitude; especially if you start to become impatient with your process. If you are unable to rise above and find true resolve you might find yourself feeding an unhealthy craving for attention and self-centered adoration. This can also resemble an indication into the deficit you hold in valuing your worth.

Tips and Helpful Hints to Remember

- Think big.
- Whatever the circumstance, keep moving forward.
- Be patient. Your process will then produce genuine success.

Be Inspired:

The birth of that marvelous wish in your soul—the dawning of that secret dream—was the Voice of God himself telling you to arise and come up higher because he had need of you.

-Emmet Fox

Meditate on this:

"...but those who hope in the Lord will renew their strength. They will soar on wings like eagles; they will run and not grow weary, they will walk and not be faint."

Isaiah 40:31

Repeat this encouragement Affirmation:

I am embracing the challenges of life. I will overcome them all.

Value Your Worth

Chapter 4

SELF ESTEEM

Too often people hold on to the negativity of past experiences. There may be times in your life where someone has doubted your ability, discouraged you or completely dismissed you. However, it is within these moments that you have the power to make a decision. You hold the power to accept or reject the things that have been negatively said or done to you. This power allows you to decide whether or not the negative things that have been said (or done) are in essence, contrary to the value of your self-worth. You may be guilty of accepting and therefore believing messages such as; "You dream too big, you're not smart enough to do that, you're not pretty enough, you think you can help people, that's a joke," and the list goes on.

The same way you delete a voicemail message after listening to it, is the same way you treat these negative commentary suggestions. Do you find yourself rewinding and replaying mean or negative experiences (messages) over and over again? What can you glean from doing this? The answer is nothing. This is self torture. It is natural that you will remember the negative things people have said or done to you. But you are not obligated to agree with the negativity that has been said, or spread. Nor is it your obligation to blame yourself for negative things that have been done. When you choose to agree and blame yourself for the negative behaviors of others, you are self sabotaging the value of your worth. In order to enjoy the life God intended for you to have, you must understand the value of your worth. This means that it may be time to start deleting those negative voicemail messages!

Morning Revelation:

School is back in session. Michelle is almost due and her seventh grade class is very excited for her. After the ring of the last bell, one of Michelle's students is still sitting at the desk. Michelle asks her if everything is ok. The student ends up crying her heart out to Michelle. She shared how she and her boyfriend got pregnant but decided not to keep the baby. Michelle's heart hurt for this girl. Michelle understood her on levels the girl wasn't even aware of. Michelle consoled the girl and helped her to feel better. Then Michelle walked her down to the school psychologist office so that she could get deepened support.

When Michelle got home all she could remember is the helplessness she saw on her student's face. It reminded her of pain identical to her past. The type of pain that she had thrown in a closet to never see again yet there it was staring in her face. Michelle became overwhelmed with feelings of exposure and tender emotion. She went from sad to angry in a matter of seconds at the remembrance of her best friend's father who had raped and impregnated her. Michelle remembered bottling the battle of wanting to tell someone, yet feeling completely incapable of doing so. As a little girl, this is why she didn't tell anyone about what happened until she found out she was pregnant.

Michelle even remembered the moment she told her mother. Her mother didn't know what to feel or say at the time. Michelle learned later on that the reason was because it spoke intimately with her own personal demons. Hence it was Michelle's mother's boyfriend who ended up taking her to the clinic to terminate the pregnancy; Michelle was only thirteen years old. As a result of such trauma, Michelle battled with low self esteem and self image. Especially after her mother sent her away to live at her grandparent's house immediately after the procedure took place.

At her grandparents house she met her neighbors Kim, Nicky, Debbie and Janice. All of whom are now no longer a part of her life after more than twenty five years of friendship.

Michelle ate her dinner in solace as the miracle of life kicked and jumped in side of her. She rubbed her stomach while realizing the baby inside could have been the by-product of low self esteem and unconfronted trauma. Michelle became conscious to the fact that it was time to work on what was now and for the first time the most important person in her life, herself. She realized the importance of how getting herself together would help her to raise a better person.

CARRYING A WORTHLESS SELF IMAGE

When you make the decision to hit the delete button to negative commentary or memories you are making the decision not to believe that the negativity held any weight toward the value of your destiny. Concurrently, you are also putting a value on your self-worth. Knowing your self-worth promotes healthy self esteem levels. The exclusivity of your self-worth is far more expensive than what people may have categorically priced you as in their limited mind space. Therefore realizing that your self-worth has far greater value than what people may price it as. It is indeed priceless.

A series of life events whether they are negative or positive, can shape how you feel about yourself. Whether you believe or reject these experiences can influence your self esteem. Self esteem does not believe only in what someone else told you about you; using what was said as the overriding definition of yourself. Self esteem is confidently believing in who you are; both the good and not so good. Sometimes you may find yourself giving people, experiences or circumstances the draining authority to define who you are and limit what you can become. Have you ever found yourself feeding into negative influences? Perhaps you have placed the opinions of others as more important than the validation you've already been given by God. God's validation means that your self-worth is deemed as valuable; valuable enough to exist. However it is up to you to believe in the esteem of your value.

PURPOSEFUL CREATION

Maybe you've been discredited or undervalued before. How did that make you feel? Are you still holding on to those feelings? Do you find yourself trying to discredit others because of how you feel deep inside? If you said yes to any of these questions you may want to self reflect upon the true level of your personal confidence. In your time of honest reflection you may find that you have believed the words of other people, or the lack therein over believing in what God through the author David has affirmed about you.

> "For you created my inmost being; you knit me together in my mother's womb. I praise you because I am fearfully and wonderfully made; your works are wonderful, I know that full well." (Psalm 139: 13, 14)

SELF LOVE

When you love yourself, there is no need to feel inferior or competitive to or with anyone else. Nowadays the mindset of comparing and competing has been disbarred by true self worth and self esteem. As a result people have become afraid to love others and afraid to love themselves. When you don't know what it means to love, it can make the idea loving yourself a very difficult concept to embrace.

Have you ever met a person who was self absorbed and enormously in love with themselves? In this sense the term love is used too loosely. Self esteem is not centered on self absorbed arrogance because arrogance does not love itself. Arrogance is an overinflated mask for insecurity within. Self esteem is the confident humble ability to love yourself and others. The ability to love yourself in a healthy perspective and share love continuously has everything to do with experiencing the love of God.

Loving yourself is not the same as vanity. Loving yourself is simply enjoying the, "you" that God made. There is not anything wrong with that. Loving yourself is acknowledging that God didn't make any mistakes when he thought about you and your life and does not compare itself to anyone else. It understands the beauty of everything in its place and has a purpose and a reason that can enable you to experience real love.

Real love vigorously challenges the soul to freely, wisely, faithfully and unselfishly give of itself. Real love is timeless and limitless in breadth and depth. It is robust in passion, intent and emotion. Once you have allowed yourself to love you, then the goal of love transforms into the ability of allowing love to flow in and through the very fibers of your being; exhausting the very essence of what you think you are or what you have become. Then real love exchanges your ability to love with a confident humility to love.

If for some reason you have not been able to love yourself with a healthy sense of self worth, now can be an opportunity to conduct a reality check. You can try believing in your value, starting today! Doing so will help you improve your self esteem.

PERCEIVED REALITY

Self esteem is a positive perception. It does not conform to meanness or spiteful intent. Improving your self esteem enhances the clarity of how you perceive yourself and can help you gain the confidence the morning introduces. Improving your self esteem occurs while keeping the right people around you. Especially in the midst of the process, it is important to surround yourself with people who truly love and care about you. It does not matter if this group of people is small in number. Their genuine concern for you is what matters most. The people who truly love and care about you will oftentimes tell you the truth about yourself. Hearing the truth about yourself will not always feel good. Sometimes it may make you feel uncomfortable. However, when it is said with love by people who truly love you, you may tend to hear the truth a little better.

Isn't it funny that when the truth is not said in love you can quickly become defensive and even ready to fight? Although the confronting individual's motive may be to take full advantage of an opportunity to rebuke you and may even be right in what they are saying, you still may not want to hear the truth; at least not from them. The reason you may get defensive in this type of situation is because there is no relationship. Self esteem is connected to love and healthy relationships. Or better yet the relationship lacks a consistent display of love. Without a relationship you might very well feel attacked. In your efforts to defend your pride from the fact that you know this confronting individual does not really care about helping you, and would rather hurt you might be opening yourself up to more hurt.

There is a scripture that makes this point of instruction more clear:

> *"Above all else, guard your heart, for it is the*
> *wellspring of life."* (Proverbs 4:23)

Therefore, be careful to guard your heart and not get side tracked by meanness or spiteful intent.

When someone is trying to hurt you, they might be mean and may do things to you or say things about you intentionally, just to see you break down. Other times a person who is trying to hurt you may really just be dealing with their own issues; possibly bred from a personal experience of abuse or trauma. For example, there are some people who bear what is called, accusatory suffering. Accusatory suffering is holding onto resentment and maintaining a victim status (Reed & Enright, 2006). Meaning this type of person feels that by holding on to the related hurt or pain they are ensuring punishment to the perpetrator and getting rightful revenge (Reed & Enright, 2006). Contrarily on a much deeper level such a person may be seen as protecting the fear that somehow they were responsible for whatever abuse or trauma may have occurred (Reed & Enright, 2006). While this may be an unhealthy reflection of how this person feels about their self, how this person feels about their self is between them and God, not them and you.

There are also people who suffer from a learned helplessness (Sackett & Saunders, 1999) and have developed patterns of self blame as a result of the criticism or ridicule they might have experienced during abuse or trauma. Learned helplessness can carry on throughout the life of the victim well past the time period of abuse or the traumatic experience (Dutton & Painter, 1993).

Any display of other people's poor self reflection and devices of accusatory suffering or learned helplessness among other things are of no consequence to you. Which means you cannot take their actions personal. You must separate yourself from their emotional distress. No matter how angry a person may be with you, you are not obligated to carry their issues, so don't! Therefore it is important to be aware of the signs that might reveal a toxic relationship. Toxic nature conflicts with a healthy sense of self esteem.

> *"...spiritual and psychological health requires a confident (but not inflated) sense of self, an awareness of human need and limitations and confiding interpersonal relationships with God and others."*
> (McMinn, 1996)

As Mark McMinn states, you can avoid toxic relationships by recognizing the signs and removing the waste of the relationship from your life.

The nucleus of self esteem purely and humbly loves itself. When you can love yourself with a healthy sense of self esteem, you will take care of yourself and be careful of your environment. Letting love in and releasing people who do not have a healthy sense of their own self, is okay. The decision to release toxic relationships is a healthy aspect of personal growth and can infuse positively healthy self esteem.

Releasing toxic people from your life will suspend the need to validate yourself through the eyes of toxins; including people and other life distractions. As you develop a more accurate perspective of self towards both the good and the not so good you can live a healthier life in esteemed gratitude. God expects that we love ourselves the way He loves us, unconditionally and interminably. In most cases this process is going to require you to have some pretty tough skin. The question is do you have it (tough skin)?

Chapter 4

Tips and Helpful Hints to Remember

- Reflect upon what may be ailing you.
- Stop embracing negativity.
- Value your worth.

Be Inspired:

Everything that happens to you is a reflection of what you believe about yourself. We cannot outperform our level of self-esteem. We cannot draw to ourselves more than we think we are worth.

-Iyanla Vanzant

Meditate on this:

For you created my inmost being; you knit me together in my mother's womb. I praise you because I am fearfully and wonderfully made; your works are wonderful; I know that full well.

- Psalms 139:13-14

Repeat this Affirmation of Encouragement:

I am wonderfully and beautifully made. My soul knows it very well.

Tough Skin

STRENGTHENED BY ADVERSITY

If you know anyone who has given birth to a child, you know that there is always a story.

Morning Revelation:

A nurse was prepping Michelle for the delivery that was underway. As the nurse began to give her the intravenous (IV) there was a problem. When the nurse tried to insert the IV, the needle broke. The nurse looked at Michelle's arm in shock. She rubbed and tapped her arm and attempted to insert the IV a second time. The needle broke again. As the nurse prepared the third and final attempt, she said to Michelle, "Wow you have very tough skin." Michelle responded to the nurse, "You have no idea!"

At this point in Michelle's life, she was profoundly encouraged by the nurse's comment. Michelle felt empowered to know that despite her life circumstances her skin was thick enough to handle what came her way and possibly the trouble that may have been on the way. The nurse's comment gave Michelle hope. It changed her mind set and ultimately changed her life.

A life changing event occurred in the delivery room. Not because of the beautiful child that she gave birth to, but because of what was spoken to her in the process of change. Her life was never the same afterward.

You might be able to identify with the feelings of embarrassment, loneliness, and isolation while experiencing a very low place in life; a place where only tough skin will get you through. Tough skin is grown through moments of adversity. Its growth is paramount the instant you can see your situation differently. The choice to see the strength that is being developed in your tough times can propel you out of a negative perspective and into a perspective that seeks to discover absolute greatness, despite the circumstances.

According to the Ohio State University Wexner Medical Center, skin is a multi-layered organism that is ever changing. It has three layers: epidermis, dermis and subcutaneous fat. These layers of skin are comprised of other multilayer tissues, glands, nerves and hair follicles. Conversely, the skin's function is to cover and protect. It covers and protects your most vulnerable organs. The most sensitive organ it protects is the heart. Having tough skin translates to covering and protecting your heart. Doing so is the secret to restoring belief in your own positive future.

Negativity can be blinding. Although one cannot erase the prevalence of negativity a person can learn how to traverse through it and succeed beyond it. Whether it be negative people or negative situations you might have created, there is a positive yang to be gleaned from what might be a negative yin. That is if you do not allow personal issues to get in the way of this revelation. Explicitly, there are two specific issues that can avert a person from developing tough skin, they are fear and insecurity.

FEAR NOT

If you are a person who lives in fear you may also be a person who lives to please everyone. Pleasing everyone all of the time is literally impossible. More importantly, if you are living a life that pleases everyone else, you are more often than not living a life that is satisfying to yourself and pleasing to God. Consequently as a result of living in fear you may have also put yourself and your entire world to include God, in a box.

As a person living life in fear your heart is exposed and completely vulnerable. Since your heart is located on the inside of your body it does not belong on your sleeve. For this reason you may find yourself in a place of compromise if you have allowed the influence of pleasing other people to persuade you away from your own personal convictions. On the other hand, when you are living a life that is on guard of your heart you are protecting your dreams, aspirations and vision that only you and God understand best.

Equally, sensitivity is very different than wearing your heart on your sleeve. Sensitivity does not have to appear as a weak flaw. Natural sensitivity can even be considered as a gift. This gift allows others to experience the grace of heartfelt compassion. Can you imagine a world with no compassion? You may already feel that you live in such a place. Nonetheless, a heart of compassion is alive in the world and is needed for balance. Tough skin is not a suggestion to eliminate your sensitive nature. The tough skin concept, allows you to consider refining it and not cut it off all together. If compassion is your gift, don't be afraid to give that. If you were to cut off your compassion or sensitivity from everyone especially if this is your gift, you may subsequently cut off a piece of who you are.

At times the attitudes of people can be a very difficult quandary to overcome. However cutting everyone off who is not like you or who does not do things the way you do them, may not be your best solution. You may have wanted to cut some people off because they really disappointed you. Or maybe they took advantage of what you had to offer. Releasing people from your intimate space and ruthlessly cutting people off are two completely different conceptions. In your reflection of the differences you may want to consider the deeper reasons why you might have thought to completely disconnect yourself from certain individuals or people all together. Has your ego been bruised? Was your pride challenged? Whatever the reason may be, the primary focus lies in whether you choose to bury the truth, allow fear to paralyze your truth or determine if perhaps insecurity is what is driving your truth. Likewise, when you choose not to deal with the real issues within, you are still cutting off a piece of you, therefore leaving your heart completely exposed as a person who has chosen to live life in fear of being free. However as the light of the morning sun begins to shine through your boxed perception, you might also begin to realize that living in fear is not living in freedom.

AN EXPOSED LACK OF CONFIDENCE

If you are a person who wallows in insecurities you may be a person who does not show their true self, so not to face the reality of the change that may be confronting you. There is no need to fear confrontation. Confrontation does not have to be negative. Many times confrontation is confused with a fight, or dispute. A confrontation is an encounter between conflicting beliefs or opinions. Confrontation is not exclusive to external reasoning. It is also available for internal dialogue. Confrontation can be experienced within one's self. Allowing yourself to pass through the uncomfortable place of confrontation will strengthen you from the inside out. You may find it easier to face confrontation with other people rather than facing it with yourself. Instead of pushing the weight of your insecurity on someone else, think about choosing to endure the process of toughening up your skin.

YOU'RE NOT ALONE

There are so many things that happen in life that can devastate your hope and put you in a paraplegic state, especially when it comes to confrontation. Have you had a negative experience with confrontation? Are you afraid to be alone? Even as bad as a situation may have hurt, or felt, or looked, God will never leave you alone. God always has your best interest in mind and will always be there for you. When you can confront the reasons why fear and insecurity may exist within, God will journey with you in the developmental growth of tough skin by looking at the real you.

Tips and Helpful Hints to Remember

- Get rid of the need for people to validate who you are and what you are doing.
- Thick skin will serve as protection when you need it most.
- Sensitivity is not bad. It gives compassionate balance.

Be Inspired:

The wishbone will never replace the backbone.

-Will Henry

Meditate on this:

Be strong and courageous. Do not be afraid or terrified because of them, for the LORD your God goes with you; he will never leave you nor forsake you.

- Deuteronomy 31:6

Repeat this Affirmation of Encouragement:

I am naturally intuitive and strong.

Mirror, Mirror on the Wall…Who am I, After All?

Chapter 6

REMOVING THE MASK

When you look in the mirror, what do you see? Do you only see your flaws, problems and issues? Or do you see beauteous peace, love and prosperity waiting to explode from within? Perhaps you see something else. Sometimes the expectation of what you would like to see can far exceed the reality of what you do see. Other times you can see the complete opposite.

SEEING PROBLEMS

Have you ever felt that as soon as you started to figure things out, things started turning into a mess all over again?

In times of frustration you may find yourself magnifying your problems to be bigger than your purpose. You may even find yourself idolizing your problems in a manner that blocks the revelation of any way out of them. The scripture advises against any form of idolatry.

"You shall have no other gods before me" Exodus 20:3

Idolatry places trust in created things rather than in the Creator. God is all powerful. He holds power over the earth, stars, moon, and the sun. Not only is He powerful, but His word is power. His word is dependable. All you have to do is make up your mind to believe it.

MIND MATTERS

Your mind holds incredible power. This is why God gives instruction in the bible, His word, on what to think. However in times of despair, worry may very well consume you. When the anxiety of your mind takes over your mirrored reflection you may be spending too much time trying to figure out solutions to your problems. When this happens, the power you hold to see and deal with the truth is abandoned. Power abandonment occurs by either masking your issues or running from them. When you run from your problems you aren't allowing yourself to go through the problem, or learn from the problem therefore ultimately you may not get to a place in your mind where you are able to grow beyond the problem. While unable to grow past your problems, you might be forfeiting the greatness that is waiting on the other side of your issue.

Problems and lack of clear solutions can sometimes become a wall and not an obstacle thus trading hope for disaster. For some, this is a crippling cycle. For others changing your problem solving strategies has a lot to do with changing your perception. The process of changing your perceptive mind begins by taking a look at the real you. It starts by asking, "Who am I?"

THE UNVEILING

In the discovery of the real you, you learn to accept who you really are so not to live your life in vain.

Morning Revelation:

Michelle is enjoying the beauty of newborn motherhood. She has worked hard at confronting her issues and growing from them so she can be a better person for herself and a great mother to her daughter. She is at peace with herself, her baby and for the direction of her life. For the first time in a long time, she prays in thanksgiving. Her prayer gets interrupted by the ring of the door bell. It is the bellman with a package. When she takes the package she opens it immediately. On the top of all of the beautiful brand new baby clothes and other baby goods there is a card. Michelle happily opens the card. "Although we can't reach you by phone, we still know where you live…Enjoy the gifts! We love you!" It was signed by the friends she had intentionally lost touch with. Michelle hasn't spoken to those girlfriends in months, so she's not sure how she feels about the gift.

A week has gone by. The gift is still sitting in the same spot she left it after opening it. Finally Michelle decides to keep the card. She mails each one of her friends a thank you card and baby picture. However, she cannot bring herself to accept the gift.

So she calls for the concierge to come and pick up the box and have the clothes and baby goods donated to the local women and children's shelter a few blocks over. The concierge arrives at her door moments later to pick up the box. She hands the box over to the concierge and then shuts the door. As she walks back to the baby's room and picks up her beautiful child, she reflects on her past and how she'd allowed it to define too much of her current situation. The gift from her friends turned out to be an excessive reminder of the past, and the embarrassment that followed her situation, so Michelle decided that she had to let all of that go. No longer would she give her past such power over her present.

It is important to accept the good, the bad, and the ugly when you look at the real you, because you cannot change what you refuse to look at. There are consequences you may face if you decide not to look at the reflection of yourself in the mirror. Furthermore there is a difference between deciding to ignore the issues you may see and when you can't see them. Ignoring your issues can be considered as being rebellious to the process of change while the inability to see the issues can be measured as being naïve to the process of growth. In either regard it is critical to your growth to face your issues once they are revealed. If you can't see any issues to work on immediately when you first look in the mirror, you may want to look again. As long as there is breath in your body, there is always growing to do!

A SECOND LOOK

The process of looking in the mirror, is taking the time to recreate definition of yourself. In accordance with the bible this does not give you the right to look down on anyone else.

"Do not judge or you too will be judged...Why do you look at the speck of sawdust in your brother's eye and pay no attention to the plank in your own eye?...You hypocrite, first take the plank out of your own eye, and then you will see clearly to remove the speck from your brother's eye." Matthew 7:1,3,5

While you are learning who you are with the help and guidance of God and through your reflection and process there is no time to judge anyone else. If you exhaust energy upon things that are irrelative and truly insignificant to the larger scope of your journey, you may find that you have no energy to deal with the things you need to confront. During this process, it is important to remember that there is no one more important than you. Get the help you need by dealing with what you see in the mirror.

SACREDNESS

Sometimes your mirrored view may be crowded with people and opinions. Throughout your journey you may discover people who do not need to be looking in the mirror with you. Some people won't understand you or the process. You may experience everything from name calling to assumptions being made or even people speaking on your behalf. Let those people talk. Just don't give them what they want. In parallel to what the scripture says, just don't give them you.

"Do not give dogs what is sacred; do not throw your pearls to pigs. If you do they may trample them under their feet, and then turn and tear you to pieces." Matthew 7:6

Your transformation is not for everyone to know about or be a part of. Many times you may feel like telling people what really is too much information, while you're still in the midst of a transition. Because of this, some people in your larger circle won't understand that you are changing. These people may not have the ability to see the absolute change until after you have completed the process. Some still won't appreciate it. In either event, that is not for you to be concerned with. Your only concern is to stay focused on looking at the real you.

TIME WASTER

In the same light don't waste time beating yourself up. Embrace your journey. Many times your journey may appear cloudy because you have been in a place of transformation for what feels like a long period of time. When you have been in a situation for a long time, your mindset can become decayed concerning what the truth is. It can also cause you to become stale in your thinking. Stale thinking may cause you to be overly concerned with what people think or will say. As a result your focus can shift away from the goal; looking at the real you.

For every day that you may have cried, endured a lie, and ate "humble pie," God knows it all. God sees the good in you even when other people do not. He knows the real you. Knowing God knows the real you is reassuring at best. God can help you through the most agonizing of issues. He will then give you the strength to face each day with a clear vision of his best intentions for you. Your journey can reveal the importance of God as your guide and can expose significance in yourself. With importance and significance comes contentment and self-esteem. Both are important to excel in life.

EMBRACE THE JOURNEY

As you begin the process of looking in the mirror it can sometimes be uncomfortable. The reflection you may see may be imperfect. Don't be alarmed here. You may cry many times. Don't be alarmed here either. Crying is releasing. Crying is the water that fuses growth. Embrace the growth don't fight it. A good cry may very well be a part of your journey, so cry and move on. Over time you will begin to look and feel completely different. If you do not see any changes, look in the mirror again… and again… and again until you see the same beautiful reflection that God sees when he looks at you.

How do you see the beauty that God sees? Seeing the beauty that God sees happens when you do not quit on the process. When you do not give up on your process you might begin to see that things are improving far beyond your expectations!

EXPECT THE GREAT

There may be times where you find yourself highly disillusioned because you may think you are progressing too slowly. Possibly you may have entered this journey with a track star attitude. However, the success of your journey is not measured by speed. No one journey is better than the other. Each journey is tailor made to the individual.

By this point, no matter how fast you may try to run away, the passion and desire to improve yourself will have already left a lasting impression. Change has been ignited. As a matter of fact it may haunt you through TV commercials, bumper stickers, and text messages. Change is inevitable. While you may have a lot of growing to do, while it is not a race, it will be most important for you to maintain your track.

Staying on track is a decision that is not necessarily an easy one to make. You may begin to feel lonely. Loneliness is a funny thing. Loneliness has a way of making you feel vulnerable. The reason you may feel vulnerability during this process is because you might be a person that has lived so much in other people's expectations that as you open up you just feel you are exposed.

Such exposure can be a sign regarding how you are living. You are not living the best life when you are living in the lane of other people's expectations and not God's standards for your life. If you know you are living within the confines of other peoples expectations, you may want to take took a long hard look in the mirror and re-define your boundaries. Allow the voids and flaws you may see in the mirror to be filled with God's love.

Have you run away from the mirror? Don't run from the mirror anymore! Let God bring you to a new level when looking in the mirror at the real you. After awhile your reflection will mature and bring you to a place where you see the greatness you have always believed was present. Then you will feel completely at ease.

Tips and Helpful Hints to Remember

- Just as Rome wasn't built in a day, change does not occur overnight. Allow your journey to be cultivated. In the end it will all work out the way it's supposed to.
- Know that you are going to make mistakes. No one is perfect, including you-and that's OK.
- Don't complain.

Be Inspired:

There is no failure except in no longer trying. There is no defeat except from within, no insurmountable barrier except our own inherent weakness of purpose.

-Elbert Hubbard

Meditate on this:

I can do everything through him that gives me strength.

- Philippians 4:13

Repeat this Affirmation of Encouragement:

May I continually grow in wisdom and understanding. I will see every problem that I face as an opportunity to learn and grow and to develop holistically.

At Ease

BECOMING OK WITH YOURSELF

You may have spent countless hours in the mirror styling your hair to ensure that every strand was in its rightful place. As you get older and have much less time or energy to spend in the mirror you may long for a more meaningful evolvement; a longing to become ok with who you are.

Morning Revelation:

> A Saturday afternoon play day had been the norm for Michelle and her daughter Melody for about eight years now. Both Michelle and Melody looked forward to their Saturday morning breakfast, a trip to the museum, and play time at the park after lunch.

At the park one fall afternoon, the sky shone a pale light. The sun was surrendered by the gray clouds waiting to seep through them. Unmoved by the clouds, Melody played energetically with her friends at the park. They ran and jumped and climbed over everything. Melody and her friends have been playing with each other for the past eight years. They were all such good friends.

Michelle watched Melody freely play her heart out. The joy in watching her daughter chiseled some of the ice that still guarded Michelle's heart from experiencing the same autonomy. Melody had not shared in the struggles of Michelle's childhood. Michelle watched the strength of her daughter rule with freedom. The purity of Melody's playtime was admiringly liberated.

Michelle smiled as she watched her daughter play. But also pondered on whether or not it was possible for someone like her to live fully in the same freedom; despite the path her journey had taken.

Michelle had worked really hard to get through the guilt and shame of childhood trauma. Only to later experience the devastation of losing what she considered to be her lifeline (her girlfriends). Michelle and her girlfriends had resolved to maintain a very surface relationship over the years. They never broke their tradition of sending one another birthday and holiday cards. However this was now the extent of their communication and friendship. Although they stopped being good friends nine years ago, Michelle had always felt the relationship was unresolved and it still bothered her, just a little.

On the other hand, watching Melody play at the park on this particular Saturday gave Michelle a new perspective. Michelle began to realize that at the point she had accepted herself and her journey she gleaned the ability to handle the context of the redefined relationship she now had with her girlfriends. Seeing the situation from a different angle opened Michelle's eyes and helped her to release in a deep sigh. She felt change occurring on the inside as the rest of the ice melted from around her heart. Finally she was ok with how things were. She was secure in herself which made everything else ok. Unexpectedly the sun broke free from the clouds and warmed the entire playground. Then, Melody ran up to Michelle threw her jacket on her mother's lap and ran back to playing, freely.

SECURITY

Security is one of the fundamental human needs, as described by the infamous Abraham Maslow's hierarchy of needs. According to Maslow's hierarchy of needs; most recognizable by its pyramid shape, he describes your basic needs to be located at the pyramid's base. Maslow's theory suggests that once a person's basic needs are met they will reach for deeper needs relative to safety and security. Maslow believed that if you do not have the basic elements of food, shelter, water, and clothing, then you will not explore the higher need for self-actualization.

SELF ACTUALIZATION

According to Maslow's theory, self-actualization is located at the top of the pyramid. A comparison study conducted by Eleanor G.

Hall and Jane Hansen on Self-Actualizing Men and Women

concluded that only two to five percent of the population ever

reaches a place of self actualization. Similar to this population you

may be striving to reach self actualization. Perhaps you have

become overwhelmed by your immediate needs and have not had

time to focus on yourself. Other times the reason you have not

reached self actualization may be related to childhood trauma. In

order to be at ease with yourself, you may just need to dig deeper

into what may be creating a block. If you can remove the block,

you can reach the goal of becoming ok with yourself.

Maybe you lacked security during your childhood or have

experienced trauma in your adulthood. These experiences may

cause you to focus on securing your environment only and deflect

from the need to be secure in yourself. Therefore it is important for

you to view the magnitude you may be appointing this need. The

danger is that you may be ignoring the need and your ability to

self-actualize. If you are not careful it can actualize in a

disproportioned manner.

One of the ways self actualization can manifest improperly is when

you suffer from post-traumatic stress disorder and trans-

generational trauma transfer. What happens when you suffer from

these mental sicknesses is that you end up grabbing for what may satisfy security in a moment of desperation rather than a more permanent life applicable solution. This can cause you to misconstrue the stamp of approval you need to have for yourself thereby looking for it in others.

LONELY LOSS

With our turning economy, you may have been a martyr to financial and emotional devastation. Possibly you are one of the many that have experienced a great loss, to include separation. Loss of a job or an important person in your life can bring about post-traumatic stress disorder or clinical depression. It can cause you to desperately crave an unauthentic security, approval, and acceptance regardless of the source. You may be trying to juggle a balance for security to make up for the lack of stability you have experienced at some point throughout your life. In addition to security, you may be looking for a sense of belongingness to avoid feeling abandoned.

ABANDONED

According to Webster's dictionary the definition of abandonment means to withdraw one's protection, support or help. It also means to throw out, throw away, and discard; to desert; to forsake; to give up completely; to leave, quit or renounce. Abandonment is a form of rejection or the loss of someone or something close to you.

Abandonment is an accumulative wound. Abandonment causes the most damage to self esteem. Abandonment and damaged self esteem yield self dissatisfaction. Unresolved abandonment can be the source of insecurities, addictions, and compulsions.

Unfortunately there is no getting away from people who will hurt you. Hurters and Haters alike come in every possible size, shape, shade, age, social form, and disposition. It is often difficult to tell the difference between who is a safe person you can trust and who is not; thereby causing deep pain.

The pain of abandonment can cause you to feel disconnected even from your own self. The cost to healing may feel like it is too much to maintain. It can also feel like it may be too complex, or more simply it may feel like the ability required superseding these feelings may overpower the ability, resources, wisdom or knowledge to grow through it. Avoiding this inner conflict will not make the strength of this need to go away. In terms of dealing with abandonment you may find the healing therein to be a cumbersome process; although, it is not an impossible one. You don't want to spend a lot of time trying to fill a void that was abandoned with painfully meaningless things.

Has abandonment made it difficult for you to maintain emotionally significant relationships? According to Maslow's theory the need for belongingness is the strongest among those who have experienced or witnessed abusive parents or have experienced neglect or ostracism. You may be craving a sense of belongingness and are trying to attach your identity to an emotionally insignificant relationship. You may be finding it difficult to maintain emotionally significant relationships because you need to have identity and contentment with yourself before a meaningful relationship can ever exist.

BELONGINGNESS

Traumatic experiences can make it difficult for you to recover, or reclaim or be at ease with who you are; especially if the trauma occurred at a young age while you were still trying to navigate through the confines of learning who you are. You may not realize it right away, but traumatic experiences can make you feel a longing to belong and feel significant. Again, you may also experience feelings of loneliness. Loneliness is not the absence of people. The reality is that loneliness is a clear representation of the absence of purpose. In order to find your purpose you will need to find a way to be ok with who you are. When you are unable to be at ease with yourself feelings of insignificance can creep in and break you down to a very lonely state. To understand who you are you must first have a relationship with God who is your Creator. Despite what you may have gone through or may be going through, your very existence implies that you do belong. It confirms that God purposed you to be here and most importantly that no matter what you may have experienced or may be experiencing, He has NOT forgotten about you!

These are only examples of some of the ways abandonment, loneliness, and belongingness may cause a distorted view of the greatness that lies within; greatness that is waiting to burst out of you. That is the type of greatness that can first be found in the beauty of being ok with yourself.

Instead of subjecting yourself to misery, deal with the drugged feelings down underneath that have the potential to exalt itself with strength. In turn the process can reveal your true identity; an identity that is not someone else's, but your own. Regardless of the battle you may be struggling to press through, as long as you are still living and breathing, there is an opportunity to find a place of peace.

Tips and Helpful Hints to Remember

- Be comfortable to be yourself before you expect others to accept you.
- Explore the sources of abandonment, loneliness and belongingness. Face and accept them.
- Get to know your greatness by getting to know your Creator.

Be Inspired:

Life isn't about waiting for the storm to pass. It's about learning how to dance in the rain...

-Vivian Greene

Meditate on this:

The LORD is my shepherd; I shall not be in want. He makes me lie down in green pastures, he leads me beside quiet waters, he restores my soul. He guides me in paths of righteousness for his name's sake. Even though I walk through the valley of the shadow of death, I will fear no evil, for you are with me; your rod and your staff, they comfort me. You prepare a table before me in the presence of my enemies. You anoint my head with oil; my cup overflows. Surely goodness and love will follow me all the days of my life, and I will dwell in the house of the LORD forever.

- Psalm 23

Repeat this Affirmation of Encouragement:

I can meet all obstacles and overcome all challenges with total confidence in my Lord, who walks with me through the deepest valleys and helps me to climb the highest mountains.

Peaceful Meadows

FINDING PEACE

Did you know that not everyone is going to like you? If you didn't know, now you do, everyone is not going to like you. Facing this fact is the type of obstacle that can present challenges to you both personally and spiritually. It doesn't matter how nice you are, how much money you have, or how good you look; there will always be someone who simply cannot stand you. Regardless of the reasons why someone may not like you, which might very well be justified, you will still need to find peace of mind.

LETTING GO

It is so easy for people to just cut other people off when you have been hurt. However, there are other ways to deal with the hurt in a manner that will enable healthy individualism. One of the ways is to simply let it go! This may be a challenge for you because the pain someone may have caused may have been very hurtful. You may be thinking, it's just that easy, eh? Just get over it? Do you know how bad it hurt? How disappointed I was? How discouraged I felt? How betrayed I was? Yes, and in order to live in peace, you will need to, let it go!

Letting go means that you are accepting the fact that everyone is just not going to like you. Acknowledging this truth will free you from needing to be liked by all. The act of letting go will move you into a place where you can dwell in peaceful meadows. It may take some time to wrap your mind around the fact that not only are there going to be people in life that don't like you, but these same people may be people you already thought you knew to be your friends.

DEALING WITH ACCUSATIONS

Have you ever been in a situation where you were being accused? Maybe this situation you were being accused of was a misunderstanding that could have easily been resolved if you just had the opportunity to explain yourself. What if, when you attempted to explain yourself, no one wanted to hear it?

Sometimes your accusers can make it blatantly clear that they are not looking for resolution. There may not be even one of them that truly care about how you feel. They now have an excuse not to like you and they are going to run with it. This can be absolutely devastating since you probably thought these people were your friends. You might have felt that if they really cared about how you felt, as you did them, then they would listen, allow you to apologize for any offenses and you'd all live happily ever after, right? Wrong. This is too easy of a solution for many. In the end you will just have to let it go. Even though it may have hurt you deeply to realize that the people you cared about for years really didn't care about you or how you felt, or better yet, lied about you in the process, you will still have to let it go. Letting go isn't easy. If you can learn to let as many situations as you can go, you can move forward with your life. Doing so will grant you access into a new place. This place is called peaceful meadows.

WHO'S RIGHT, ANYWAY?

So many times excuses are applied to situations instead of applying peace to them. For example you might say or think, well if he/she didn't say that in the first place, I wouldn't have had to give him/her a piece of my mind. Giving everyone a piece of your mind is like aiding and abetting a criminal. Neither one of you will get off the hook until someone faces the responsibility of the offense. Within the strategies of confrontation, there is a fine line between initiating resolution and starting trouble. On the other hand, staying away from drama is always a sure retort.

At the end of the day it doesn't matter if you were the one right in the confrontation and they were wrong or vice versa. Being right or wrong is irrelevant to people who don't live in peaceful meadows. These people feed off of the negative energy of arguing a point to a pulp; never reaching any resolution or reconciliation. Even still, you have to let it go.

Morning Revelation:

Michelle is standing in the mirror with her third dress on. She wants to make sure she is wearing the right dress for her hot Friday night date. With Melody now off to her third year of college on a full academic scholarship Michelle is a proud mother, excited and confident woman who is still extremely nervous about the dating scene. Thankfully she has been seeing a very handsome gentleman for seven years and counting. He is just downright dreamy.

As she stood in the mirror and began to think about her date's handsome debonair status she quickly changed into her fourth ensemble. Only to realize she is now running late. She runs to the elevator and hails a cab to the restaurant.

Michelle arrives at the fancy restaurant about ten minutes late. The host brings her to the private table her date had reserved. He was always such a gentleman. She orders a glass of wine to calm her nerves. She thinks this may be the night she's been waiting for. "Will tonight really be the night I get my ring?" Michelle is happy in her thoughts as she gazed into the glass of wine. Twenty minutes have gone by, so she steps away from the table to call her date on her cell phone and see if everything is ok. His phone picks up on the first ring, "Hey" he responds, "Yes, How are you?" Michelle found his response to be oddly unaffectionate but didn't pay much attention to it. Michelle is too excited for what may happen and does not want to ruin the moment with antagonizing questions. But she does ask, "Are you close?" "Well sort of, I am stuck in traffic but I'll be there as soon as I can, baby." There was still something very strange about how he sound. But she said, "Ok. I'll be waiting." and hung up.

As Michelle walked back to the table she noticed he had arrived and was walking about two people in front of her. She could recognize his walk anywhere by the length and smoothness in his strides. While she knew it was him she didn't say anything. She thought it was very sweet that he was about to surprise her since he had just said he was stuck in traffic. Then she watched him turn left headed to the table. This presented a problem because getting to their table would have required that he turn right. So she began to slow down. Then her feet froze. They wouldn't take another step. Her eyes were in shock as they stared at her man kiss another woman and sit down. She didn't know whether to cry or scream or run away. So she captured the moment. She took a few pictures on her cell phone and left the restaurant.

Michelle arrived home in a very calm mad. Maybe it was still shock, but she didn't feel the need to go crazy, whereas ten to fifteen years ago might have been a completely different story. Michelle's boyfriend had a key to her apartment. The original plan was to have dessert and coffee after dinner at her place. So she was expecting him to return there.

Michelle is sitting in the dark by the window in the living room. He comes into the apartment foyer whispering on the phone. Clearly he thinks she is asleep since it is dark. She just listens. Finally Michelle gets up and goes to the kitchen turning on the light. "Mike, is that you?" "Yes, darling what an awful accident" he says as he comes to kiss her on the forehead. "I'm sorry I couldn't make dinner. I went by the restaurant and the host said you were gone." "I wasn't going to wait forever, especially when the rest of the night wasn't over yet. I knew you'd come by for a nightcap. I have dessert still, have some with me."

Her boyfriend sits down at the island bar in the kitchen while Michelle pours coffee and prepares dessert. She serves him the dessert and coffee while asking, "So where was the accident?" He choked on his coffee. "Oh man, that went down the wrong pipe;

can I have some water please?" "Sure." Michelle got the water and brought it to him. Mike began to tell a very elaborate story regarding the accident. Michelle knew he was lying and couldn't stand it anymore so she interrupted him abruptly. "Oh, I almost forgot. I have something to show you." He gets excited. "Should I close my eyes?" "You can, but I'm going to text it to you. Let me get my phone from my bedroom. I'll be right back." Michelle goes to her bedroom and sends the picture text messages to Mike. With her phone in hand she goes out to the front room.

For some strange reason the picture messages were taking a long time to send. He began to get anxious. So she sent them again. "Are you sure you sent it? What is it? Is it something I'll like to see...like you" "Yes...I'm surprised you haven't gotten it yet. I'll send it again." "Ok." "But Mike, Let me tell you honey, the picture is worth a thousand words." After about ten minutes, the pictures hadn't yet sent. So he begged her to show him what she sent, but from her phone. She didn't give in that easily. Partly still in shock, she wanted him to see and have the pictures on his own phone. They playfully wrestled for her phone and he tickled all of her favorite places until finally she agreed to show him the pictures from her phone.

Romantically entangled on the couch Mike's face went pale when he saw the pictures. He quickly sat up and rubbed his head in disbelief. Michelle reaching for an answer in his mind let a tear run away from her eye and down her face. Mike stared blankly at the pictures as his six foot three inch figure arose from the couch. Then Mike's phone went off about seven times. It was the same pictures over and over again that Michelle had previously sent. "Michelle..." She stood up in a five foot six statue and covered his lips with her index finger, "Shhh." Mike tried to hug Michelle, but she told him, "No." He took a deep breath, removed the key to her house from off of his key ring and put it next to the half eaten dessert and coffee. Then he grabbed his coat and looked at Michelle and said, "Baby, I'm sorry." Michelle turned around and faced the window because she didn't want to show him any more grief and she didn't want to hear anymore bogus explanations. Instead she said, "Please leave my key and don't call me again." Mike did just that. He walked out of the door never to return again.

Michelle took a deep sigh. Then she cried and released Mike from her heart. As crazy as his departure was, Michelle was proud of her response. It was the reality of how much she had grown over the course of time. She walked away from the relationship in tremendous peace as a true victor and not taking the familiar role as a victim.

Stop giving people so much power over you. So what if people lied on you or lied right to your face. Stop wasting time and energy trying to correct every little thing someone has said about you or done to you. By doing this, you are wasting YOUR life! Holding on to all these types of excuses as a reason not to live in peace is only holding YOU back from enjoying a peaceful existence.

Understand that you do not owe anyone anything. It is pointless to argue with a fool. Finding peace has nothing to do with politics or being polite but rather it is all about you finding harmony within yourself. Some have mastered the art of social politics, but have completely failed at truly having rest in their soul. Even if your so called friends have failed at truly finding peace, you don't have to.

DEFEATING THE ODDS

Do you know that when you find peace, true peace, you completely defeat your enemy? What is an enemy you say? An enemy can be someone who calls themselves your friend or an enemy doesn't have to be a person at all. An enemy can sometimes be intangible. An enemy can be an attitude, a lie you can't control or address or even the bitter broken heart that can't stand to see you enjoying life. But guess what, you win the battle with the enemy when you choose not to fight, but to find peace!

Think about the moment you find out about the lies and wicked things that someone has assumed and spread about you. Imagine that this person called themselves a friend, or even a relative and has no idea that you know what they said and spread about you. Adding insult to injury, this isn't even the first time that you know they've done it! What if a secret you shared in the deepest confidence was just exposed! What do you do? Naturally your initial inclination is to be hurt and disappointed. After that you will probably feel anger or become enraged depending upon your issue. With all of the burning emotion surging through your body, what do you do? You let it go.

EMOTIONLESS DECISIONS

Too many times emotions are allowed to overpower people. If you are one of those people who make emotional decisions constantly, you could be making terrible choices that are feeding the fire of your emotions rather than quenching them. You feed the fire of your emotions when you whine to all of your friends, co-workers, and other people about your feelings in a manner that poisons the potential of your own healing. Doing this also brings toxins into any current relationships. These toxins not only destroy other relationships, but also can cause wreckage on your path to finding peace.

It is true that there are times you need a sounding board on a particular scenario. It is healthy to vent. It is unhealthy when your venting is driven by bitterness. Are you reaching for vengeance instead of reaching for help? If you are not careful, bitterness can turn into slander, all under the disguise of venting. The goal is to avoid turning into a "bag lady" that carries slander as a protective weapon. Such a woman or man holds bitterness at the core. Don't allow the pain of bitterness to choke you. It will cause you to die and you will never experience true peace within.

Do not miss interpret this to be a rant on dismissing emotions. In fact, emotions are very real. You don't look at emotions like a movie, you experience them. You feel them and from these feelings, your emotions manifest. However reckless emotions will leave a clear path to destruction all around you and create a self implosion if they are not dealt with. In either case, you will still need to find peace through the adventure of your emotions.

Other situations where peace is found require you to simply admit that you are wrong. No one is right all the time. The stroke of the ego always feels good, but the building of good character which at times can be uncomfortable comes through humility in peaceful meadows. Accept that you are wrong and move on.

In most cases, pride is hard to swallow. Don't be tricked into believing that holding onto hurt, pain and vengeance is benefiting you. Therefore:

"Do not take revenge, my friends, but leave room for God's wrath, for it is written: "It is mine to avenge, I will repay," says the Lord." Romans 12:19

God will take care of the situation and in turn, it's okay for you to let go. Letting things go into the hands of God converts your weakness into strength and will enable you to have the wherewithal to pick yourself up and move to a place of peaceful meadows.

A peaceful meadow is more about a decision than it is a location. Regardless of the circumstance or how tumultuous the devastation, there is a path to peace. It is your choice to forgive and forget- meaning not holding on to the emotion attached to the situation, let go and keep it moving. This process is divinely cultivated through the break of the dawn of illusion.

Chapter 8

Tips and Helpful Hints to Remember

- Deal with emotions honestly.
- Search your heart, mind and soul for areas of un-forgiveness. Then, forgive and forget.
- Surround yourself with positivity.

Be Inspired:

The fragrance always stays in the hand that gives the rose.

-Hadia Bejar

Meditate on this:

You will keep in perfect peace him whose mind is steadfast, because he trusts in you.

- Isaiah 26:3

Repeat this encouragement Affirmation:

True peace is a reflection of my inner man. I am peace because I am at peace.

The Dawn of Whirlwind Illusions

Chapter 9

BELIEVING THE TRUTH
ABOUT YOURSELF

If someone says to you, "that looks nice on you," do you believe the compliment given, or do you try to find excuses as to why the compliment can't be received? Are you the person that responds, "Oh, this old thing" instead of saying "thank you?" Often times when you choose not to believe the truth about yourself you will find yourself in a whirlwind of illusion.

WHEN IT'S ALL A SHAM

Living in a whirlwind of illusion is a formula for a disastrous breakdown. Maybe you have already had a personal breakdown. Or maybe you thought you were having a personal breakdown when really your breakdown was based on the fact that you could no longer keep up with the counterfeit ideals you put in place to satisfy your own unrealistic expectations. Negative life experiences may have helped you to design unrealistic expectations according your environment to include the opinions of others. In either regard, creating such expectations adds on the pressure to become something you are not. This can cause you to feel anxiety about filling in the gap between who you show people you are, what you've chosen to believe you are, who people told you are, and who you really are. As a result you may have created a person who longs for admiration for something you only wish you could be.

Do you wish you could have a, "you parade" where everyone is cheering in constant adoration for you? Wouldn't you love to hear the parade first thing when you wake up and continue through the night? Can't you see the drum major leading the way? Aside from potential annoyance, this notion is unrealistic. If you didn't see anything wrong with the idea of having a constant cheer squad follow you around, you may want to consider your need for adoration. Maybe you are looking for such an immense level of admired support because you've been told that you are a failure so many times that now, you believe it. Perhaps you have found yourself in a place where you are hungering for confirmation and affirmation. If this is true, then you may be using the parade to ward off or drown out the sound of negativity you have chosen to believe in an attempt to feel a sense of confirming affirmation about yourself. A counterfeit success has the job of tricking you into believing a lie. For this reason, what the parade cannot do is make you believe in a more positive reality of self. You have to believe the reality of a more positive truth, on your own.

REJECTING NEGATIVITY

You are living in a whirlwind illusion if you allow yourself to become a puppet in subjection to the influence of other people's negative realities. Becoming a puppet to negative realities is comparable to embracing the pessimism once or maybe repeatedly said to you and translating these things to have value in your life. For the very fact that you are reaching out for a team of support to counter the negative ideals that have infiltrated your way of life, proves that the power you have within is probably being neglected. This means that somewhere deep down inside, you may know the negative you are embracing is not the truth. The negative is not your reality in the sight of God either, even if it is a real part of your current situation.

Embracing the negative is a remedy of simplistic human knowledge. When your human knowledge ignores God it magnifies your problems because the answers to your problems cannot be found without God's eternal perspective and solution.

God's eternal perspective and solution is to believe. That is to believe in Him and believe in yourself. If you choose to operate in your human knowledge alone, then all of your wisdom is a vain pursuit of meaninglessness. At which point you are then living in an illusion. If you are finding yourself trapped by a lifestyle of a whirlwind of illusion you are probably a person who believes your present day reality defines who you are. Better yet, you may also believe these realities are the boundaries of limitation to who you can become. The fault in believing this is that there are no limitations to who you can become. Have you been the person halted by hallucinate limitations? If so, you may want to consider breaking the dawn of whirlwind illusion.

BREAK OF DAWN

In order to break the dawn of whirlwind illusion you must begin to see your reality in the state of the future and not in the state of your present. Instead of believing in a permanently false reality, challenge yourself to question your perception and ask what you can do to improve your reality. If you can be honest about where you are in the illusion process, then you can honestly change your mind. Recognizing this truth can transform the way you see yourself and provoke change even ahead of the actual change event. This may be a new dimension of thinking for you and that's ok. Thinking beyond another level and into a new dimension can

motivate a renewed perspective when it comes to the
transformation of whirlwind illusions.

Transformation doesn't have to take a long time. You can find
yourself beginning the changing process and transforming the
perception of your life in a matter of seconds. While the process
takes time the moment of change doesn't have to take years,
months, or weeks to achieve. The onset of change occurs at the
moment you decide to think differently and then begin to practice
it. The only thing required from you in the process of breaking the
whirlwind of illusion is a willingness to accept the fact that what
you have believed is not the reality of truth. On the other hand,
sometimes ego can get in the way of your change event.

It is natural for your ego to seek the path of least resistance
because the ego is ignorant to the fact that there is no permanence
in the idea of easy unless it is self created. Narcissistic behavior
only sees and is motivated by itself. What you must be careful of
throughout your transformation is allowing your ego to deceive
you into believing that the change process is too hard or
impossible. The illusion of impossibility is broken when you take
responsibility for your reality. Breaking such negative illusions
requires faith.

"Now faith is being sure of what we hope for and certain of what we do not see." Hebrews 11:1

"Now" faith is declarative and speaks to the present. It is also affirmative. Secure faith trusts God completely and does not require any signage. Have you ever prayed for a sign or some indication that you are on the right track with the vision for your life? If you already can see the vision for your life and its endless possibilities, what do you need a sign for? The need for a sign reveals that you have lost hope in the promise. This means that you are questioning the promise of transformation. At which point you may be filled with doubt and no longer believe in its occurrence. While your faith is absent in this moment, it can be found. Although to find faith, you must first know what it means.

Faith is not an illusion; it is factual belief in what your natural being may see as impossible in the present. Faith forecasts potential and sees it as real. This is why faith is an essential ingredient to believing the truth about you. Faith is emotionless in its conviction; it believes confidently and doesn't need the validation of other people to affirm or confirm its purpose. Faith will help you to see beyond your past or present circumstances and allow you to look through the mirror at the you, you can become.

Plausibly, you may not be where you want to be in life right now. Maybe you are still beating yourself up about the choices or mistakes of your past. Did you know faith doesn't see you in the past? Faith is forward thinking at its finest! Faith holds you accountable to greatness without blaming the incapability's of your consciousness on the limitations of your environment. Instead, faith allows you the opportunity to take yourself beyond the capabilities of your physical, emotional or mental state; breaking you out of assumptive and constrictive self made solutions of hopelessness.

A GLIMPSE OF THE MORNING

Can you see yourself with faith enough to tear down the walls of the hopeless despair that you put up brick by brick? Without faith you are blocking the light of the morning. The wall and the clouds within your whirlwind illusion can block you from seeing that. To overcome this and activate faith you can try a new approach. This new approach involves self examination. Examine yourself and ask what the greatest expression of yourself is and how can you maintain it. Then, memorize this feeling. The thought and faith in the greatest expression of yourself and the path to maintain it, is transporting the real you to the forefront. By dismissing the addictive behavior of embracing the negative, you are bringing to the surface the person who you really are. The success of this process is determined by a choice. You can either see yourself going through this change successfully or you can decide to remain an addict of negative illusion.

ADDICTED TO THE GLIMPSE AND NOT THE LIGHT

What is an addict you say? An addict is a person who is controlled by an activity or substance despite any harmful consequences. When a person is under the influence of their addiction they have activated a chemical in their brain called dopamine; a neurotransmitter that releases pleasure. This type of pleasure may come with feelings of clarity, relief, or the fulfillment of being invincibly at one with the universe.

According to the Harvard Health Medical Publication on addictions, when an addict is engaged in the action of their addiction where they are satisfying a need or fulfilling a desire, a signal is produced that says to the addict, not only does this activity feel good it is subsequently providing a feeling of reward. From a medical stand point this system of thinking is called the reward pathway. For a moment the reward pathway makes the addict believe everything is wonderful. Worries may disappear and for once, the addict may feel as if every part of their life is in its rightful place. Even if just for a moment this substance or activity allows the addict to disconnect from the concerns of the past or the future. This moment of highness allows them to only be concerned with the good feelings of the present.

The Harvard Health Medical Publication on addictions also states that the repeated use of drugs shuts down the brains ability to produce dopamine naturally. As a result the addicts' desire for the addiction increases in order to try to fill in the gap between expectation and reality, even physiologically. As the addict continues to overwork the functionality of chemical releases within the brain, the brain is then losing its access to think about other, although less immediate, yet powerful sources of reward. This means that the addict loses their sense of personal control and begins to believe that they need the substance or activity in order to survive. What this does is take away the mechanical ability to self enthuse the act of change. This is why the addict craves the substance or activity even when it no longer gives them pleasure.

An addict then is on a mission for immediate pleasure. They are always looking to be ok, right now and in the present. Therefore an addict is a person who truly desires to be present. Psychologically, the addict demonstrates a content to process shift when they abuse substances to please or fulfill emptiness. Therefore it can be acknowledged psychologically, that the addict is looking for presence; significance and meaningfulness. Unfortunately an addict has allowed a whirlwind of illusion to convince them that they do not have presence or they only have presence under the influence of the desired substance or activity. Similar to an addict you may feel as though you are in a dark whirlwind of illusion. If so, try to remember that sometimes growing through a dark place can allow you to realize the empowered light of change. Within this journey you must determine what matters to you.

Otherwise you can miss out on the vast potential to be birthed out of what seems to be a dark place. When you are ready, this type of change starts with turning the light on. With the light on you can see the power that learning, consciousness and repetition has within the formula of true change. During your process let this light shine on your whirlwind of illusions so that you can recognize those illusions for what they are, a figment of your imagination. Once you navigate through the tresses of your dark imagination then you can find the positive and live out the rest of your life loving yourself, believing the truth about who you are, and having the faith in your continued evolution.

Morning Revelation:

Saturday seems to be a day of riding the waves of emotionalism. Michelle started to do her normal Saturday Yoga routine, but she still felt incomplete.

She stopped doing Yoga and started doing the laundry until she ends up pouring bleach into the load of colored clothing. Frustrated she goes to the roof of her sky rise to lay in the sun by the pool. She found solace in being alone and on top again, even if it were only in symbolism. Michelle lay in a bed of disbelief, "How could Mike be so insensitive? Why not just break up?" she thought, "After seven years why cheat, now?" She almost started to release a good purging cry until a group of her neighbors and their friends came up to the roof top to enjoy the nice weather and pool. "Hey Michelle, join us!" "No, that's ok; I was just heading back downstairs. Have fun!" "Ok Michelle, but next time, you owe us!" Michelle smiled and gave them a thumbs-up. She went back to her apartment because nothing seemed to calm her up to this point.

Michelle sat at her window seat and prayed. Through prayer she told God how she feels painfully distressed. After prayer she decided to read the bible. Clumsily she went to pick up the bible and dropped

it. It fell open to a familiar passage of scripture,
regarding Gods love. She chuckled at the scripture
and felt that was God's way to show her that he was
right there with her, loving her because He really did.
Believing that God loved Michelle was exactly the
love she needed at exactly the right moment, now.
She clutched the bible close to her heart, remembering
the God of her youth. Remembering the God of her
grandparents and realizing the depth of love in God
she had just re-found. Michelle let her head fall back
and closed her eyes in comfort. She fell asleep at the
window as the morning sun warmed her face
through the window pane.

Are you afraid to change? Don't be. If you can, begin to shift your
gears to the next level through self actualized and enlightened
awareness and let the sunshine of a new morning break the dawn
of whirlwind illusion. If you choose not to, then you may find
yourself living in fear of what God has planned for you simply
because you are not thinking big enough. Think bigger. Believe
you can break the dawn of illusion and live fearlessly!

Chapter 9

Tips and Helpful Hints to Remember

- Reject negativity.
- Find, increase, and or restore hope and faith.
- Embrace the light of change.

Be Inspired:

Gold is found in the dark.

-Unknown

Meditate on this:

"Jesus replied, "I tell you the truth, if you have faith and do not doubt, not only can you do what was done to the fig tree, but also you can say to this mountain, 'Go, throw yourself into the sea,' and it will be done."

Matthew 21:21

Repeat this Affirmation of Encouragement:

I believe what I say am, ignoring all of the negative contrary to this truth.

FEARLESS

Chapter 10

KNOWING YOUR AUTHORITY

Many people have fear of the unknown. That is why some of you have been sitting on a business, a book, a music project, television idea, or ministry for years. As you exit from one new beginning to another, you cannot be afraid of what lies ahead. During this time in your life you will explore several transitions. In the end, you can evolve into a new person. The moment of each evolution will call for you to be fearless!

Morning Revelation:

On her way back from Melody's grand destination wedding, Michelle is overwhelmed by mail. One of the letters caught her attention in particular. It is a letter from Nicky. However it was not the normal Holiday Greeting card so Michelle thought something may be wrong and opened this letter first. In it was a long letter asking for forgiveness and requesting if they could all meet for lunch like old times. The letter included Nicky's contact information. The letter further explained how everyone ended up going their separate ways and that Nicky realized she was the cause of the majority of the turmoil that had been experienced amongst their group of friends. Michelle couldn't agree more since Nicky had always been somewhat of a trouble maker. What did surprise her was that Nicky had actually admitted to it and apologized. The letter from Nicky included her phone number. Michelle has a mixture of thoughts after finishing the letter. But her primary thought is to decide whether or not this is good for her. A lot of time has passed. Michelle was a different person. "Could Nicky be different, too? What if she wasn't? What about the other girls?" Michelle thought. Michelle prayed and then felt comfortable responding to the invite.

Michelle text Nicky to say, "Got your letter, I'll be there." Nicky replied, "Thank you. I'll see you soon."

Later that week Michelle gets to the restaurant and sees Nicky sitting in the restaurant alone. Michelle stood outside and watched Nicky through the restaurant windows glass wall for quite a few minutes. From across the street Michelle watched each friend walk in one by one. Michelle was hesitant but knew she had to go in. As she walks closer to the table Michelle questioned her motives, thoughts, and intentions. Only five steps from the table, Michelle takes a deep breath, releasing fear and trusting God and her decision. She sits to down and greets her old friends.

Releasing fear has a lot to do with trust. Many times people have learned that it is safest to trust in themselves and not in anyone else. Not even God. As a result you may be reasoning in your mind to find a logical exchange. Unconsciously, what you are doing is bargaining and sometimes compromising purpose for fear. You may have found that your spouse or friends or family are not dependable. This may have inflated your ego to believe that you don't need any help because you can do it all. It's safer that way, right?

Who knows, maybe you can do it all. However, you'll need to realize that releasing fear is not about your ability, alone. A fearless mentality is about recognizing the authority that has been given to you. Without this acknowledgement, your efforts alone are powerless.

KNOWING YOUR AUTHORITY

Power was transferred to you the day you were born; the power to dream, the power to dare and the power to challenge yourself to grow. Life situations can sometimes aid in this power slipping completely from your grasp. But what God does to restore this power is He gives you the morning. He gave you this morning to meet yourself and realize who you really are; who he's created you to be. He wants you to realize the authority you have in Him. This authority is fearless in success and abundant in possibilities. Your authority is most clearly expressed through submission to God's will. Submission to God's will frees you to obediently operate in the power given you through your relationship with God. Your relationship with God is best expressed when you revere the establishment of his authority. God is the utmost power source. What this means is in the order of power, is that God comes first. When you put God first, all else will align itself properly. Obedience to this principle is the highest expression of your willingness to trust God's will because it omits your personal opinion from the equation. It removes the, "I only trust me" factor and reflects definitive trust in the superiority of God.

SUBMITTING TO CHANGE

It may not be easy to come to a place of submission. Childhood trauma can paralyze your ability to submit to God. It can strike fear into people who feel they have the toughest of hearts. After facing the real you and all of the issues in between you will learn how to have a voice. If you hadn't felt this before, you'll be able to feel it and for some, feel it again. What makes this difficult to compute as it relates to submission is because you may have never felt before. You may have gone through things so devastating that you learned to suppress your feelings. You may even be afraid to feel because all you have ever felt was pain. In the pursuit of a fearless nature and either restoration or resurrection of the real you, you are going to have to feel the good and the bad. You may even feel joy and pain all at once. In either regard you still have control because when you submit to God's power you are resting in his hands. You trust his guidance. Don't choose to rebel against it. When you choose rebellion, really what you are choosing is the desire for you to be in control rather than letting God be in control. This is a formula for fearful disaster.

You may find that post childhood trauma and into adult hood that to hear your own voice may be refreshing. When you hear the power in the sound of your voice you can experience the influence that you have in the universe. The power you hold in this moment can command destiny to manifest right before your eyes.

Do you fear what would happen when you let go of expired people, places and things in your life? Where would you be without them? After long, these questions can plague your mind. Your mind can become your worst enemy. This enemy can be what holds you back in fear. The enemy both spiritual and carnal does not want you to get to the place where you recognize the authority of God and the power therein. The enemy or enemies want to keep you from moving forward. For that reason it is detrimental to your process to ensure honesty is maintained with yourself about yourself.

DENIAL

There is no room for denial on your journey. The longer you remain blinded by denial regarding your own self righteousness the longer it will take for you to face your fears. Therefore you will never make it to the path of true destiny. This type of mindset will only further deter and distract you from realizing your God ordained fearless authority.

Sooner or later the real you may catch up with any imitation version of yourself that you put on display for everyone else to see. You may feel like you are in control, but really, you are powerlessly in control. Your reign of control may lead to many battles within. You may find yourself fighting your intuition tooth and nail about the people, places and things that it is just time to let go of. Actually when you do this, you are living in fear of the unknown. The move from fearful to fearless means that you to step outside of yourself and trust in God to lead you into the greatness that lies ahead. The greatness that lies ahead will remain untouchable if you never make a decision to change your perception from fearful to fearless.

FEARLESS NATURE

Despite overwhelming situations, you were not created to be afraid of anything. You were created to move, live and flow in the abundance of love, power and sound mind. Don't ever let people; circumstance or failures convince you otherwise. You were made to live in the representation of your Creator, the King, and the true and living God. His power is the ultimate authority given to you so that you may soar in peace, health and prosperity. So go for it - whatever "it" may be. Maybe "it" is a new business deal, or a different job, starting school, or a new friendship. Don't let fear keep you from living the full and complete life God wants for you. Take a moment to reflect upon your trust level in God. Do you fear the unknown? If so, try a new approach; try to trust God without fear or having to know the next step. In exchange for fear, God will give you the type of courage that supersedes resources, relationships or the guilt of past experiences. You will begin to see life in an entirely positive perspective.

Without fear the glass is not half empty, it is half full! Everything you see will be half full and waiting on your contribution to it. All you have to do is be fearless. As a matter of fact give fear an eviction notice! Besides, with God as your guide, what is there really to be afraid of anyway?

Chapter 10

Tips and Helpful Hints to Remember

- Give fear an eviction notice!
- Recognize God as the source of power.
- Recognize your power.

Be Inspired:

He who has overcome his fears will truly be free.

-Aristotle

Meditate on this:

For God did not give us a spirit of timidity (fear), but a spirit of power, of love and of self discipline.

- 2 Timothy 1:7

Repeat this encouragement Affirmation:

I will live freely and fearlessly.

SPARKLE

Chapter 11

THE MORNING GLOW

EXPERIENCING THE NEW YOU!

As the cliché goes, diamonds are a girl's best friend. Diamonds are worn around the finger, wrist and neck of women all over the world. Today diamonds are a marveled after for their beauteous sparkle. But did you know that those beautiful diamonds began as a lump of coal? Diamonds are formed approximately one-hundred feet below the earth's surface. Through supersonic volcanic eruptions from the earth's mantle, diamonds are dejected to the surface. When a diamond is found, it is a rock that looks like a lump of coal. The coal surrounding the diamond is dirty, dusty and shapeless. So then, how does the diamond get its sparkle? A diamond gets its sparkle from enduring the process.

The diamond's structure is what makes the rock and the process so different. It's made of various elements of carbon. The arrangement of its carbon atoms and carbon to carbon bonds generate its strength. Diamonds can withstand great pressure and extreme heat. It isn't until the rock endures an intense amount of heat and pressure that it becomes the wondrous luxury it is today. Often times, you may go through a similar process in life. If you do, you must endure your process.

ENDURING THE PROCESS OF TRANSFORMATION

Sometimes when you're going through your process, you may not know what to say! There are times where devastation happens so fast that it can leave you completely speechless. Even so, there is no need to freak out. It is an absolute must in your process for you to use the resources God has made available to you. It will be too easy to abort your destiny without using them.

"Surely, LORD, you bless the righteous; you surround them with your favor as with a shield." Psalm 5: 12

In this scripture King David is praying to God about his consternation toward the lies spoken about him by his enemies. God is able to defend and protect you with his favor, even from the lies that may have been spoken against you. The favor of God is not exclusive to houses and cars and money. God's favor is supernatural. God cannot be put in a box. The flows of favor in your life can indeed mean new houses and expensive cars, but it also speaks to the intangible things you cannot see, hear or touch.

There is no reason for YOU to be walking around sad or mad things didn't turn out the way that you had planned or that there are people believing things about you that are not true. To your benefit, Gods protection will manifest itself to the natural realm and He will keep you safe even in the heat of your process. You don't have to go through your process by yourself.

JOURNEY PARTNER

If you were meant to work out your life's journey by yourself, God would have put only one person on this earth and that would have been you. He didn't do this because people need each other and more importantly people need God. When time gets tough in life or while you're in your transformation process, you will need a rock. You may need to be able to lean on something dependable. Liken to a particular scripture:

> *"God is my salvation and my Glory: the rock of my strength, and my refuge is in God."* Psalm 62:7

You may also need to learn how to depend on God as your rock, especially in these times.

Your support system may include good friends, family or a spouse. All of these are important, but God should be the rock to it all. You cannot replace God with a junk food support system. If you do, you are then starving your purpose. God is that rock that is your primary source of strength. Sometimes "Mama and them" aren't available, are no longer living, or just can't cut it. What do you do then? Know where your strength comes from. God is your perfect strength throughout the duration of your transformation process.

In this life there is no one that is perfect, so stop trying to be. Doing so puts too much pressure on you unnecessarily. Furthermore, adding tremendous amounts of self inflicted pressure may reflect inward and might cause sickness and disease. Let go of the idea of perfection and retire the habit of making excuses for what you are not. Whatever it is you are trying to be consider the fact that maybe you are not supposed to be. Maybe you are only supposed to be yourself. Stop trying to be something you are not. It is what it is and what it is is your process. Don't worry; you'll make plenty more mistakes in life. Learn from each one and remember it is all a part of the process.

BEYOND THE SURFACE

During your process, make it a habit to observe what's going on around you and in your circle. Be sure to examine the areas in your life that need changing, tweaking or adjusting. When those adjustments involve people it is important to understand that people come into your life for a reason and a season and it is up to you to ask God, what they are there for, before you let them in. You may not always choose people wisely, but you can remember that God knows what was best for you. He knows when a relationship is not healthy for you and your growth. Be obedient and release relationships that have no substance. You may find that you might be looking for companionship or friendship in the place of finding self. If so, what you're searching for is far deeper than any man or woman can fulfill. In reality more times than not, your craving is for an appetite only God can fulfill; self discovery. Be careful to allow only God to fulfill your appetite. Otherwise you can end up searching the world for something only he has to offer. Doing it Gods way will prevent much heart ache.

Like the diamond, your journey may be tough, rough and crushing. It may create a core of scurrilous and unbearable pain. Instead of going crazy, choose to be at peace. Being "at peace" with God is not a "feeling," but rather is a condition opposite to enmity. Meaning that God is investing time in changing YOU and how you deal with your circumstances instead of just changing your circumstances. The benefit to you in looking beyond the surface is seeing beyond exterior improvements and seeing the evolution of permanent transition. So be strong and courageous to endure; don't quit. Whatever you may be experiencing, this too will pass. With God on your side, front and back you are bound to come out of your process shining.

VICTORIOUS SHINE

Sparkling victory may not necessarily be about reaching a destined place more than it is about arriving at a place of peace with your journey; which begins with an awakening. In being yourself there is no effort required. You come fully equipped with your own original sparkle.

The morning you met you is representative to the event of a self awakening. It is the event of change. Your awakening can begin in an accelerated sunlight or slow dreary day. In either case, your awakening is the morning you meet you. It will be the key to freedom from continuous stress and pressures to live outside of the skin you're in.

Morning Revelation:

To her surprise, Michelle is having a great time. It's almost as if those bad times never existed. Everyone has matured, just like she did. They spent the afternoon sharing their journey's experiences and laughed at all of the silly things they thought was so important, which now have tremendously less value.

Michelle excuses herself to the powder room. On her way back, she notices a familiar face. Mike has just walked in the door. Michelle's heart skips a beat. She hadn't seen him in years and he still looks good. He began to walk towards her. Mike complimented her as he always did. He said he admired her sparkling glow and was glad to see her. Michelle obliged his comments as he followed her back to her table. Michelle introduced him to her friends. They loved him. He made them all laugh. Michelle noticed something different in him also, even if she didn't say it aloud. She felt it was good to see him. He looked well and at peace. Mike's comment resonated with her, "I admire your sparkling glow." In the midst of all of the laughter it was at this moment Michelle felt herself sparkling.

Michelle looked at her hands, she knew they sparkled. Not because she felt better than any one of her friends at the table nor was it because she restored a healthy relationship with her old friends. Michelle believed she sparkled because she had at last become ok with herself and was confident that God would always have her best interest in mind. She enjoyed the day with her friends. When she got home she noticed she had a voice message on her phone. It was Mike, "It was really good to see you Michelle. I'd love the opportunity to talk and take you out for coffee. If you're interested let me know." After hearing the message Michelle smiled. Then the doorbell rang. Michelle opened the door and it was the bellman with a box of long stem red roses from Mike. Michelle was flattered but decided to pray before her emotions got too attached to the idea of dating Mike all over again. "Could he be trusted?" Michelle asked. Although she fully intended to accept the warm displays of an apology,

Michelle wanted to please God more than any other decision to move forward in re-opening the door to having a relationship with Mike. She had learned a lot along her journey and understood that pleasing God would lead her to ultimate happiness. Alternatively Michelle was perfectly fine with letting go of Mike if that was what she needed to. For guidance, she prayed, "Lord I trust you. I am awakened by your light and love. Lead me and I will follow you. Amen." After praying Michelle was confident in leaving the balance of her life in God's hands and was at peace with the path God lead her, whether it involved Mike, or not.

Open your eyes, its morning! Today marks the day true personal and spiritual transformations takes place. It marks the place where you are not afraid of what is going to happen in the future. Your awakening is meeting you and loving what you see, every step of the way. It is realizing that the day that life begins, happens on the

day you stop caring about what doesn't matter. This day sparkles
with love and light. This day, is "The morning you meet you!"

Chapter 11

Tips and Helpful Hints to Remember

- The victory of destiny is not necessarily about reaching a destined place, more than it is about arriving at a place of peace with your journey; which begins with an awakening.
- Whatever the circumstance, keep moving forward.
- But be patient. Your process will then produce genuine success.

Be Inspired:

Authenticity is the unique nature of contentment.

-Yolanda Lewis

Meditate on this:

And without faith it is impossible to please God, because anyone who comes to him must believe that he exists and that he rewards those who earnestly seek him.

- Hebrews 11:6

Repeat this encouragement Affirmation:

It is through God's grace that he is leading me to achieve my highest good, today and forevermore.

SEALING THE DEAL

Chapter 12

A TIME TO PRAY

Heavenly Father I graciously position myself before you humbled by your love and mercy; new mercy that you've given with the new day. I am thankful. I am asking for a special blessing to rest upon those who have read this book and hear your voice. Allow the words that have been spoken to cause the type of "springing forward" that will invoke inner transformation in the lives of your people.

Thank you for bringing each and every reader to the morning they will meet you (and themselves). Dear Lord, please protect their decision to journey in the new morning. Please saturate the atmosphere of every circumstance with your holy power.

Your name is the sweetest I know. And your love is amazing. Lord your name is above any other name we could call on for help. It is in your name, that I believe miraculous things can happen. I also believe that you are hearing our prayer right now and are working on the readers behalf, even as we speak.

Lord, please send the reader of this book peace and restoration. Together, we praise you now for healing, deliverance and freedom from addictions, hopelessness, fear and doubt.

I stand in agreement with the reader of this book that only you know the heart of. They need you Lord, like we all need you. Please show them in a peculiar way that you love them and have not forgotten them.

We thank you Lord, for the everlasting love in every new beginning. We pray together and seal the rest of our lives with peace and prosperity. We give you all the praise for these things in advance.

Amen!

Hello Morning!

Don't miss these other titles by:

YOLANDA LEWIS

Available for order at:

www.extreme-overflow-enterprises.com/products/

References

1. Inspirational Quotes. (2012)
   http://www.beliefnet.com/Inspiration/Inspiration-
   Quotes.aspx#ixzz221piR0fl

2. Margarita Tartakovsky, M.S. 5 Tips to develop thick skin
   (1998-2012)
   www.pscychcentral.com/blog/archives/2012/07/06/5-tips-to-
   develop-thicker-skin

3. Ohio State University-Wexner Medical Center: Anatomy of the
   skin (2012).
   www.medicalcenter.osu.edu/patientcare/healthcare_services/sk
   in_conditions/anatomoy_skin/Pages/index.aspx

4. Harry J Gaynor, PhD. The American Academy of Experts in
   Traumatic Stress, Inc. (1998)
   www.aaets.org/article63.htm

5. The American Heritage Dictionary
   www.thefreedisctionary.com

6. Raymond Lloyd Richmond, PhD. A Guide to Psychology and
   its Practice. (1997-2009)
   www.guidetopsychology.com/reltx.htm

7. Eleanor G. Hall, Jane Hansen. Self-Actualizing Men and
   Women-A Comparison Study. (1997).
   www.positivedisintegration.com/Hall1997.pdf

8. Cate Lineberry. Diamonds unearthed (2006)
    www.smithsonianmag.com/science-nature/diamond.html

9. The people Vs the state of illusion (2004)
    www.thestateofillusion.com

10. Elizabeth Hartney (2011), What is an Addiction.
    http://addictions.about.com/od/howaddictionhappens/a/defaddi
    ction.htm

11. Harvard Health Medical Publications (2004)
    http://www.health.harvard.edu/newsweek/The_addicted_brain.
    htm

12. Berke JD, et al. "Addiction, Dopamine, and the Molecular
    Mechanisms of Memory," *Neuron* (March 2000): Vol. 25, No. 3, pp.
    515–32.

13. Crabbe JC. "Genetic Contributions to Addiction," *Annual Review of
    Psychology* (2002): Vol. 53, pp. 435–62.

14. Hyman SE. "A 28-Year-Old Man Addicted to Cocaine," *Journal of
    the American Medical Association* (Nov. 28, 2001): Vol. 286, No.
    20, pp. 2586–94.

15. Hyman SE. "Why Does The Brain Prefer Opium to Broccoli?"
    Harvard Review of Psychiatry (May-June 1994): Vol. 2, No. 1, pp.
    43–46.

16. Koob GF, et al. "Neurobiological Mechanisms in the Transition from
    Drug Use to Drug Dependence," *Neuroscience and Biobehavioral
    Reviews* (Jan. 2004): Vol. 27, No. 8, pp. 739–49.

17. Nestler EJ. "Total Recall – the Memory of Addiction," *Science* (June 22, 2001): Vol. 292, No. 5525, pp. 2266–67.

18. Austin Vickers (2009)
http://www.austinvickers.com/corporate/human-process-mastery-trainin

19. McMinn, M. R. (1996). *Psychology, theology, and spirituality in Christian counseling.* Carol Stream, IL: Tyndale House.

20. Reed, G.L, Enright, R. (2006) The Effects of Forgiveness Therapy on Depression, Anxiety, and Post traumatic Stress for Women After Spousal Emotional Abuse. *Journal of Consulting and Clinical Psychology*, Vol. 74, No. 5, 920-929

21. Sackett, L. A., & Saunders, D. G. (1999). The impact of different forms of psychological abuse on battered women. *Violence and Victims, 14*(1), 105–117.

22. Dutton, D. G., & Painter, S. (1993). The battered woman syndrome: Effects of severity and intermittency of abuse. *American Journal of Orthopsychiatry, 63,* 614–621.

Made in the USA
Charleston, SC
10 March 2013